# BREAK THROUGH

## DISCOVERING
## GOD'S POWER
## FOR YOUR
## PROBLEMS

**NELSON SEARCY**
with C.A Meyer &
Jennifer Dykes Henson

Published by Church Leader Insights U.S.A.

Printed in the United States of America

    Library of Congress Cataloging-in-Publication Data
Searcy, Nelson
    breakthrough: discovering god's power for your problems / Nelson Searcy, C.A. Meyer and Jennifer Dykes Henson

    p. cm.
    Includes bibliographical references. ISBN 978-1-7363541-6-2
    1. Religion—Christian Life—Spiritual Growth

*Dedicated to all who are stuck, hurting, suffering, uncertain, purposeless or facing challenges of any kind and are seeking God's solution for their problem. Get ready for your BREAKTHROUGH!*

# TABLE OF CONTENTS

Reader's Note: This book is co-authored,
but the book's tone is written in Nelson's voice
for consistency. Assume all stories are Nelson's unless
otherwise stated since—as we jokingly say—
he's had more problems in life!

# INTRODUCTION

There's a word for one problem after another after another: *life!* We're always in one of three places: in the depths of a current problem, on the steep road out of a problem, or on the descent into the valley of a new problem. As discouraging as that may sound, we've all lived long enough to know that life is full of issues and difficulties. They simply come with the territory of living on this side of heaven.

Contrary to what some people think, being a Christian doesn't exempt you from having problems any more than being an EMT exempts you from having accidents. I'm a long-time Christian and I have problems. I had problems before I became a Christian and problems after becoming a Christian, though once I trusted in Jesus, my most significant issue—a problem concerning eternity—was fixed! But more on that later.

The fact that you picked up this book tells me that you, too, have faced problems in life. You may be facing one right now. I've been there—over the years, my family has faced health issues, financial concerns, homeowner nightmares, relational disappointments, unexpected setbacks and unending trials I'd rather not relive in print. But writing this book has forced me to think back to some of those experiences. I'll mention a few because maybe, just *maybe*, you can relate:

- Early in my career, I owned a computer business. My largest account refused to pay me, kept my original work and essentially told me, "You'll have to sue us to get the money." *Problem!*

- After moving to a new town, I was living on a very tight budget. I had to take my car to a nearby garage to address what I thought was a minor issue. The minor issue turned into an almost $2,000 expense. *Problem!*

- At age 45, when I was by all measures in the best physical shape of my life, I was diagnosed with stage 4 cancer. This obviously became the biggest problem I've ever faced.

Within days of my diagnosis, I had the first of multiple surgeries. My doctor told me to expect to live for about six months unless chemotherapy or some miracle breakthrough extended that timeline. Gratefully, by age 48, I was cancer-free! My cancer is gone, but post-cancer problems persist and probably will for the rest of my life.

---

Is your problem stealing your joy?
Your strength? Your courage to keep going?
God sees you. He sees your struggle.

---

If you're facing a problem right now, know that I can relate to a lot of what you're feeling. That leads me to ask: Is your problem stealing your joy? Your strength? Your courage to keep going? God sees you. He sees your struggle. You can be confident that He is with you through anything this life may bring. Deuteronomy 31:6 says:

*So be strong and courageous! Do not be afraid and do not panic before them. For the LORD your God will personally go ahead of you. He will neither fail you nor abandon you.*

Everywhere we look in life, there's brokenness—that's the reality of living as broken people in a fallen world surrounded by other broken people. But no matter what you're going through or how terrible your situation is, Jesus offers hope. The Bible is filled with wisdom and encouragement for you. Despite what you may feel in the moment, you *can* be strong and courageous when the storms of life hit.

You *can* be strong and courageous when you lose your job.

You *can* be strong and courageous when you go through a breakup.

You *can* be strong and courageous when you find out a loved one's health is at risk.

You can be strong and courageous *because* God goes ahead of you in any and every circumstance you face. He will never abandon you—*never*. Do you believe that? Do you face your problems like you believe that?

This book is my challenge to you: Instead of trying to live a problem-free life (which is impossible), look to God for His help through the inevitable problems you will face. Turn to His Word for guidance on whatever situation you're in. Learn how to live for eternity even now and how to never lose hope, no matter what you're facing. Those things *are* possible.

Unfortunately, many people don't believe they can live a life of hope rather than one of stress, struggle, and pain. I'm convinced one of the reasons for that unbelief is that they've bought into dangerous culture-cultivated myths about God and the life He's given us.

If you buy into these myths instead of God's truth, your problems will defeat you. So, before looking at the Bible's solutions to our problems, let's address the lies culture would like us to believe.

## MYTH #1: LIFE SHOULD BE PROBLEM-FREE.

Many people are shocked when difficulty shows up on their doorstep. But Jesus clearly told us that life on this earth would be full of problems.

> *I have told you all this so that you may have peace in me. Here on earth you will have many trials and sorrows.* (John 16:33)

Even if you love God, love others and strive to do everything in life according to God's Word, you're still going to encounter the pain of problems. Jesus wasn't a sinner like us—He lived His life on earth in total, perfect obedience to His Father—and still He faced some of the worst problems of all. If we believe the myth that our lives are supposed to be problem-free, we're always going to be discouraged. We're going to doubt God's goodness. We're going to continually ask, "Why is this happening to me? Why are You allowing it?"

As humans made in God's image (Genesis 1:27), we ache for heaven's perfection—for all things to be good, right and fair. But none of our lives will be problem-free on this side of eternity. Thankfully, Jesus went on to give us this promise:

> *But take heart, because I have*
> *overcome the world.* (John 16:33)

The sooner you accept that problems are an unavoidable part of life, the sooner you'll be able to see what God is doing in you and for you through the problems you face. His strength and courage will help you stand in the face of whatever comes—and not only stand but also have joy and peace when it makes no sense for you to have those things.

---

The sooner you accept that problems
are an unavoidable part of life,
the sooner you'll be able to see what
God is doing in you and for you through
the problems you face.

---

## MYTH #2: EVERYTHING (EVERY PROBLEM) HAPPENS FOR A REASON.

People say this all the time, thinking God is orchestrating every good and bad thing that has ever happened to them. But God is not the author of evil. He didn't create it, and He doesn't weaponize it against us. He *does* allow us to go through difficulty with good—albeit at times mysterious—reason, but we can always trust He has a plan. We can trust that, as our loving Father, He is always drawing His children closer to Himself. And that's exactly where we should want to be.

God is never manipulating the circumstances of our life with harmful intent. Believing that lie leads many people to resent Him. When we start to resent God, we alienate ourselves from the strength, comfort and peace He offers us in our pain. Although not easy to accept, it's usually our own sin, someone else's sin, our sin-riddled world, or a combination of all three that cause our problems. Even so, we have hope. As Jeremiah wrote:

> *"For I know the plans I have for you," says the LORD. "They are plans for good and not for disaster, to give you a future and a hope."*
> (Jeremiah 29:11)

God can take whatever you're facing right now and work it out for good in your life. That's His specialty. He brings good out of evil, hope out of despair and life out of death. He didn't cause your problem, but He will use it.

## MYTH #3: NO ONE UNDERSTANDS YOUR PROBLEMS.

If you think no one understands your problems, you're buying into a myth that can trick you into believing you're alone. The author of Hebrews wrote this about Jesus:

> *This High Priest of ours understands our weaknesses, for he faced all of the same testings we do, yet he did not sin. So let us come boldly to the throne of our gracious God. There we will receive his mercy, and we will find grace to help us when we need it most.*
> (Hebrews 4:15–16)

Look at the scars Jesus bears if you think no one understands what you're going through. He knows the problems you're facing. He's deeply familiar with the hurt you're feeling. Even though He is God, He was also completely human. Jesus endured the most agonizing death on the cross when He died for our sins.

Not only that, but He has placed people around you who can relate to your pain, even if they haven't faced the same exact circumstance you're facing. If you allow them, they can walk with you alongside the Savior.

Here's our hope: Jesus rose from the dead! He defeated sin and death. And if He can overcome the power of sin and death on the cross, He can help you break through whatever problem is overwhelming you right now.

## EXPERIENCING A BIBLICAL BREAKTHROUGH

No matter the problem you're dealing with, God can bring a breakthrough. Take a look at my working definition of a biblical breakthrough:

**A *breakthrough* is when God grows you deeper in your relationship with Jesus, through the power of the Holy Spirit, by providing a biblical solution to the problem you're facing.**

God has a solution to every problem you face. He is never stumped, and He always has your best interests in mind. In the pages ahead, we're going to explore biblical mindsets and tools that, when applied through the leading of the Holy Spirit, will allow you to access God's solution—your breakthrough—for your problem. The result of every biblical breakthrough you experience will always be a closer walk with Jesus.

For now, remember this: the danger with the three myths listed above is that wrong belief always leads to wrong action. False ideas about God, yourself and life's problems lead to sinful responses to pain, which make everything worse.

---

The result of every biblical
breakthrough you experience will always
be a closer walk with Jesus.

---

The truths we'll uncover in the chapters to come are not quick fixes, and they're not always going to be easy. But together, with God going before us, we can discover how to be strong and courageous as we go through (and grow through) life's problems, continually relying on our faithful Father to bring our breakthrough.

*Do not be afraid or discouraged. For the*
*LORD your God is with you wherever you go.*
(Joshua 1:9)

(For additional resources related to this book, including supplemental material, group study guides, related audio teaching, author contact info and more, see www.Breakthrough-Book.com.)

# GOD'S POWER IN A PROBLEM

*Jesus Feeds the Four Thousand*
Matthew 15:32–39

Then Jesus called his disciples and told them, "I feel sorry for these people. They have been here with me for three days, and they have nothing left to eat. I don't want to send them away hungry, or they will faint along the way."

The disciples replied, "Where would we get enough food here in the wilderness for such a huge crowd?"

Jesus asked, "How much bread do you have?"

They replied, "Seven loaves, and a few small fish."

So Jesus told all the people to sit down on the ground. Then he took the seven loaves and the fish, thanked God for them, and broke them into pieces. He gave them to the disciples, who distributed the food to the crowd.

They all ate as much as they wanted. Afterward, the disciples picked up seven large baskets of leftover food. There were 4,000 men who were fed that day, in addition to all the women and children. Then Jesus sent the people home, and he got into a boat and crossed over to the region of Magadan.

## CHAPTER 1

# WHAT NOT TO DO WHEN YOU HAVE A PROBLEM

While you likely picked up this book because your problems are *real* problems, I thought it would be an interesting—and humbling—start in our journey together to take note of some *first world problems* common to many of us. Then we can get serious.

Common First World Problems:

1. The phone charger cable not being able to reach your bed

2. Losing the TV remote

3. Not being able to skip the ads on live TV

4. Slow Wi-Fi anywhere

5. Forgetting your password

6. Being hungry but not for any of the food in your fridge

7. Forgetting where you parked

8. When it's your turn to unload the dishwasher

9. Cracking your phone's screen

10. Pouring your cereal before realizing you're out of milk[1]

We all have plenty of these not-so-problematic problems. But not all our problems are this trivial, are they? Now that we've had a little fun, let's get serious about the real problems in our lives.

## LEARNING WHAT NOT TO DO

Your first step is to learn what *not* to do about your problems because, as I've mentioned, when you mishandle the difficulties that arise in your life, it leads to more difficulty. And if you're already feeling

---

1    CollegeTimes Staff, "32 Ultimate First World Problems That Everyone Faces," https://www.collegetimes.com/entertainment/ultimate-first-world-problems-90543.

distant from God because of your problems, multiplying those problems could cause you to push Him further away.

Take Adam and Eve, for example: When they sinned, they hid the shame of their sin by covering themselves in animal skins and hiding from God (Genesis 3:8). God called out to them, but they continued to hide, thereby further distancing themselves from their Creator. They had an initial problem, and their response to that initial problem created more problems. Sometimes the cover-up is more problematic than the crime.

Or take King David. He pursued Bathsheba even though she was someone else's wife. Not only did he lust after her and then act on his temptation, but David kept sinning to the point of sending Bathsheba's husband to his death on the battlefield (2 Samuel 11). Ultimately, David's series of terrible decisions in response to his initial problem led to increased heartache for his entire family line.

Leaving God out of your problems because of shame, pride, or misdirected anger will only lead to even more worry, frustration and pain. But if you bring your problems to God, no matter how big or small they may be, you can have His peace—peace that Jesus bought at a high price on the cross for all who trust in Him. Even if your circumstances don't miraculously change, your heart, mind and perspective will (Philippians 4:7).

---

Leaving God out of your problems
because of shame, pride, or misdirected
anger will only lead to even more worry,
frustration and pain.

---

Unfortunately, we're often too quick to try to solve our own problems—like Adam, Eve and David—before turning to God. As a result, we usually make things worse. But we can choose to approach our problems differently, starting now, by making sure we're aware of the three big *What Not to Do's* when trouble comes our way:

1. Don't turn away from God.

2. Don't get bitter.

3. Don't give up.

(For further reading on how to remain strong during life's problems, pick up a copy of my book *Unshakable: Standing Strong When Things Go Wrong*. See Appendix E of this book for a sample chapter. To secure a copy visit www.Breakthrough-Book.com.)

## DON'T TURN AWAY FROM GOD

If you buy into one of the myths listed above, you will be more likely to blame God whenever you face a problem. Eventually, your grievances will begin to build on each other, and you could get mad enough at Him to walk away from what you know to be true.

Turning away from God is the worst thing you could do in the face of a problem. Turning away from God means turning away from your strongest ally, the One who loves you most and the One who holds the breakthrough for your problem. By turning away from Him, you're essentially ensuring that what you're facing will overwhelm you.

The wisdom and power of the One who created the universe are more than enough to cover whatever you're struggling with right now. His response may not be what you want, or in the timing you'd prefer, but you can always trust that He's there for you to lean on and to comfort you far more than any human ever could. As Psalm 46:1 says, "God is our refuge and strength, always ready to help in times of trouble."

I've been a Christian for a long time, and I still surprise myself by how long I can go between the time a problem hits and when I remember to lean into God. The distance between those moments can be embarrassing. For example, the IRS once audited me. And let me say, no matter how sure you are that you've done everything right on your tax reporting, your stomach drops into your toes when that letter arrives. Mine certainly did. My fear drove the decisions I made that day:

I opened the letter.

I stewed about the letter.

I told my wife about the letter.

I stewed about the letter some more.

When I finally looked at a clock later that afternoon, it was too late to call my accountant. I worried through dinner.

I took my English bulldog for a long walk to try to settle down. (Note: English bulldogs are great dogs, but endurance walkers they are not!)

That's when the answer hit me: *Maybe you should lean into God on this. Stop coaxing your bulldog for another block and pray. Seek God's peace.* That walk with my dog transformed into a talk with God. But why did it take me so long to get to that point? I'm human.

I've seen this pattern in others' lives too, both new believers and mature Christians. It always goes something like this:

1. A problem occurs.

2. You complain to a friend/spouse.

3. You vent about it on social media.

4. You worry and lose sleep.

5. You allow it to impact your mood and close relationships at home and work.

6. You may even skip your small group Bible study because of the headache the problem has caused.

7. If you make it to church that weekend, you're distracted and can't focus on worship.

Sounds unproductive, right? In fact, it sounds downright destructive. And it could all be avoided by taking the right first step when a problem arises—turning to God instead of making the mistake of turning away from Him. We must discipline ourselves to turn to God *first*. His power and presence are essential.

This reminds me of a great classic hymn. Although I didn't grow up in church, I have a great appreciation for hymns, those praise-filled songs with endlessly relevant insights into the daily happenings of our lives:

*What a friend we have in Jesus,*
*all our sins and griefs to bear!*
*What a privilege to carry*
*everything to God in prayer!*

*O what peace we often forfeit,*
*O what needless pain we bear,*
*all because we do not carry*
*everything to God in prayer!*

*Have we trials and temptations?*
*Is there trouble anywhere?*

*We should never be discouraged;*
*take it to the Lord in prayer!*

*Can we find a friend so faithful*
*who will all our sorrows share?*
*Jesus knows our every weakness;*
*take it to the Lord in prayer!*[2]

God is ready and waiting to receive any hurt, anger and confusion you surrender to Him in prayer. If you turn to Him in your time of need, He will

---

2    Joseph Medlicott Scriven, "What a Friend We Have in Jesus," 1855, public domain.

encourage you with His loving presence. As James 4:8 promises, "Come close to God, and God will come close to you."

## DON'T GET BITTER

We've all seen it, haven't we? Something difficult happens in the life of a family member or friend and they begin to change. They begin to question their faith. Sometimes, it seems to happen overnight. Maybe you hear them make a bold declaration of unbelief, words said in anguish or unfiltered rage. More often, it happens over time. A gradual sense of bitterness begins to seep into their minds and hearts until the problems in their life become their god and resentment becomes their form of worship. God Himself gets displaced by anger, misery and pride. If you've seen this happen, you've likely told yourself that you'd never allow yourself to go down the same path.

But then something difficult happens to you—maybe a series of difficulties. Slowly, you feel a bitterness you never wanted creeping in, ready to rob your joy and peace. My simple, biblically consistent definition of *bitterness* is "anger or disappointment—often at God—for feeling you've been treated unfairly." Be on guard not to let such anger or disappointment gain a foothold in your heart. Hebrews 12:15

warns, "Watch out that no poisonous root of bitterness grows up to trouble you."

No matter how overwhelming it may seem, when you face a problem, you have a choice: you can get bitter, or you can allow the problem to make you better. The only way to get better is to lean into God's healing love. He can work through that problem to make you stronger, more courageous and more patient. Only He can use it to change your perspective, grow your character and enrich your soul. (For deeper study on avoiding bitterness and other emotional pitfalls, see my book *The New You: A Guide to Better Physical, Mental, Emotional, and Spiritual Wellness*. Learn more at www.Breakthrough-Book.com.)

---

No matter how overwhelming it may seem, when you face a problem, you have a choice: you can get bitter, or you can allow the problem to make you better.

---

We just want our problems to go away, but God wants to use them for our growth and His glory. He *is* using them. So instead of praying, "God, make my life easier," we should be praying, "God, make me better. I know there will be obstacles in my life, but make me strong enough, courageous enough, to stand face-to-face with whatever this broken world throws at me, knowing it's You who keeps me upright." Jesus said in John 14:27:

> *I am leaving you with a gift—*
> *peace of mind and heart. And the peace*
> *I give is a gift the world cannot give.*
> *So don't be troubled or afraid.*

With Jesus, we have the gift of peace over panic. We can trust that He will use our trials to make us better if we'll lean into Him.

## DON'T GIVE UP

Too often, we give up on things God has called us to by claiming we need a change. For example:

- Your exams are too challenging, and you're almost failing that one impossibly difficult class, so you take the "Withdrawal" status and change your major to something else. You tell everyone that you just felt the need for a *change*.

- That dream of owning your own business requires far greater effort and time than you thought it would, so you decide to move toward a different profession instead. In reality, you're giving up, but you call it *making a change*.

- Your marriage isn't going well, and you're not feeling as in love with your spouse as you used to. So you move out, saying you both need a *change*.

---

With Jesus, we have the gift of peace over panic. We can trust that He will use our trials to make us better if we'll lean into Him.

---

Don't get me wrong, there are times when change is a good, necessary part of life. But unfortunately, our culture tries to bait us into making changes like the ones above whenever something seems difficult. The world would call these changes brave, but that attitude—that when things are hard, we should avoid the hardship and seek our own comfort above all else—factors God out of the equation. Worse, it belittles the reality of His power to do incredible things in and through our hardships.

Most of us are conditioned to want to operate within our comfort zones. We do all we can to avoid stress, problems and unnecessary pressures. But the thing is, we don't grow when we are comfortable. Often, it's the most uncomfortable things in life that grow us the most. We get stronger when we go through the discomfort of lifting weights. We run farther and faster when we go through the pain of pushing beyond our previous limits. And God often grows us by allowing and using circumstances that make us uncomfortable. The term used to describe stress that leads to positive change is *eustress*. Unlike distress, eustress is a type of beneficial stress that ultimately leads to a greater good.

While we certainly don't want to live in a constant state of stress, eustress can be a useful tool to help grow us into the people God wants us to become. When we experience eustress, our character grows. Our faith grows. Our ability to handle similar situations in the future grows. What used to send us into distress, now moves us into the eustress zone instead. We become capable of handling more and doing more for God. That's why it's critical that we don't give up when we face hard times. We can't run away from the difficulties in our lives. We must grow through them to find God's best on the other side.

(For recommended resources on managing stress, see www.Breakthrough-Book.com.)

---

> While we certainly don't want to live in a constant state of stress, eustress can be a useful tool to help grow us into the people God wants us to become. When we experience eustress, our character grows.

---

Just think, if God had given up on humanity when it became obvious how difficult we would be to deal with, none of us would be saved. None of us would have the incomprehensible gift of knowing Him as our Father. None of us could call out to our Savior, who so obediently called out to His Father in the garden of Gethsemane the night He was betrayed, saying, "My Father! If it is possible, let this cup of suffering be taken away from me. Yet I want your will to be done, not mine" (Matthew 26:39). But God didn't give up on us when things got hard. Quite the opposite, He gave Himself up for us.

I pray that we would remember this every time life's problems tempt us to give up. Let's hold on to the truth that even though suffering may crowd our lives with sorrow, we can be at peace, encouraged and even joyful in our pain. The very thing we're all most afraid of, that phantom terror lurking at the corners of our comfort, didn't defeat Him. How Satan must've raged. Echoing some of the suffering Jesus endured leading up to the cross, Paul wrote:

*We are pressed on every side by troubles, but we are not crushed. We are perplexed, but not driven to despair. We are hunted down, but never abandoned by God. We get knocked down, but we are not destroyed. Through suffering, our bodies continue to share in the death of Jesus so that the life of Jesus may also be seen in our bodies.* (2 Corinthians 4:8–10)

Did you catch that last part? Through our suffering, we get to "share in the death of Jesus so that the life of Jesus may also be seen in our bodies." Like Jesus, believers are brought from death to life. The life of Jesus is in us, equipping us. So why would we ever give up?

---

But God didn't give up on us when things got hard. Quite the opposite, He gave Himself up for us.

---

Maybe this truth seems impossible to believe given the problem you're facing right now. Maybe you can't imagine how things could ever get better for you. But with God, a breakthrough is possible (Matthew 19:26). Commit to doing your part by turning toward Him, refusing to get bitter and not giving up.

(P.S. My IRS audit came back clean, but I'm still learning the lessons of this chapter.)

## TAKE ACTION FOR YOUR BREAKTHROUGH NOW

See the "30-Day Breakthrough Worksheet" in Appendix A to more clearly identify your area of breakthrough and to begin a 30-day process that you can utilize in parallel with the upcoming chapters. For a download of the worksheet, see www.Breakthrough-Book.com.

# GOD'S POWER IN A PROBLEM

### *Jonah's Prayer*
Jonah 2:5–10

"I sank beneath the waves,
    and the waters closed over me.
    Seaweed wrapped itself around my head.

I sank down to the very roots of the mountains.
    I was imprisoned in the earth,
    whose gates lock shut forever.

But you, O LORD *my God,*
    snatched me from the jaws of death!

As my life was slipping away,
    I remembered the LORD.

And my earnest prayer went out to you
    in your holy Temple.

Those who worship false gods
    turn their backs on all God's mercies.

But I will offer sacrifices to you with songs of praise,
        and I will fulfill all my vows.
        For my salvation comes from the LORD alone."

Then the LORD ordered the fish to spit Jonah out onto the beach.

## CHAPTER 2

# PRAY, THEN PRAY AGAIN

We say we want God to help us with our problems. We say we want His direction to deal with them and His endurance to help us walk through them. But as I mentioned in the previous chapter, He's often the last one we turn to.

Typically, we turn to our friends first. Godly friends who can provide wise counsel are important—and there is a time we should turn to them—but going to them before we go to God with a problem we're facing can be dangerous. They're human like us, and the fact that they're our friends usually means they're invested in us. They are likely to take our side even if we're in the wrong. And if we're turning to friends who don't know God, that's even more dangerous. People who don't seek the will of God themselves are not going to encourage us to seek it.

Next, we turn to our family—our spouse, parents, siblings, or grown children. But our loved ones, too, are biased. Whatever situation we're facing is likely something they're also entrenched in, either directly or indirectly, through their relationship with us.

Third, many people turn to therapy by reading self-help books, Googling coping techniques, or meeting with a Christian counselor. As helpful as those options may be, if they're *all* we're turning to, we're forgetting the Counselor and Comforter God has gifted all those who believe in Him—His Holy Spirit. Thankfully, the Holy Spirit does not have office hours; we can meet with Him anytime.

Recently, I (C.A.) noticed how often I go to other people before I go to God. When an unexpected problem arises, my fingers habitually reach for my phone before I think of who I'm about to call or text. If it's a big problem, sometimes I'll call or text several people, usually copying, pasting and sending the same message to my closest friends one after another for their input. But in the solitude of waiting for their replies, I realize my error. The panicked tempo of my heartbeat can steady only with God's help.

Instead of looking up to talk to Him, I'm looking down at my phone to seek advice and comfort from everyone else. And when my friends reply, their responses—though filled with love and truth and encouragement—are filtered by their own opinions and experiences. Although well-meaning, they could unknowingly lead me away from what God's calling me to do, as I could them. But God offers me His wisdom directly when I go to Him with my problem in prayer.

My (Nelson's) working definition of *prayer* has always been that prayer is simply "talking to God." In this case, prayer is talking to God about your problems. Some people are afraid or ashamed to do this, thinking things like *I don't want to tell God about this problem*, *I'd be ashamed if He knew*, or *It seems so small* (as if there is such a thing as a "small" problem). Or, out of ego, they simply want to handle it themselves. But when you talk to God about your problem, He's not surprised. He already knows all about it and is just waiting on you to turn to Him and ask for His help. He will *welcome* your turning to Him (see James 1:5).

---

When you face a problem,
don't go to the secondary sources first.
Go to the expert, our all-powerful God.

---

Think of it this way: If you had a toothache, and that tooth was close to rotting and could cause worse health issues if you didn't handle it correctly, would you call your friend to complain? Or your family member so you could cry to them in agony? Or would your first call be to your dentist so you could receive specialized help and begin the healing process?

It's the same in your spiritual life. When you face a problem, don't go to the secondary sources first. Go to the expert, our all-powerful God. No matter how much other people love you, God created you, breathed life into you and sent His Son to this earth for you. God did this so that you could be reconciled to Him. Why would you turn anywhere else when you have a need? No matter what you're facing, run into the arms of your Father first. Go into a quiet room, close the door and talk to Him. Philippians 4:6–7 says:

> *Don't worry about anything; instead, pray about everything. Tell God what you need, and thank him for all he has done. Then you will experience God's peace, which exceeds anything we can understand. His peace will guard your hearts and minds as you live in Christ Jesus.*

Let's unpack the implications of this passage. Notice in the first sentence that you have a choice when a problem hits: you can either worry or pray. One of my mentors used to say that worry is stewing without doing. We are so prone to stew over problems and let them dominate our thoughts. But which is going to help more—worrying or praying?

The second sentence says, "Tell God what you need, and thank him for all he has done." We know how to tell God what we need. No problem there. It's the *thank him* instruction that catches us by surprise. But that's not just a nice addition Paul threw in; there are several applications of how thanking God is critical when we are tempted to worry. Here are two:

1.  Thanking God for what He has done gives you the opportunity to look back and remember God's faithfulness in the past. When you thank Him for His help with your past problems, you grow in confidence that He will help you again.

2.  Thanking God on faith that He is going to address your current problem in His time and according to His will increases your trust in Him. Even though the breakthrough God is going to bring may not be clear to you yet, it's clear to God. He already has a path set out for you, one that will help you *grow* through—not just *go* through—the difficult circumstance you find yourself in.

The last sentences of this passage are profound: "Then you will experience God's peace, which exceeds anything we can understand. His peace will guard your hearts and minds as you live in Christ Jesus."

Talk to God. Thank Him for all the ways He has proven Himself faithful in the past. Trust Him to do it again. This doesn't mean your problem will immediately disappear, but it does mean that your anxiety will lessen as you grow in God's grace. When God chooses to provide a breakthrough amid your hard circumstances, He will do it in a way that will draw you closer to Him. A biblical solution to your problem is always one that will deepen your walk with your heavenly Father. As you call on Him in faith, His peace will surround and comfort you.

Go back and reread Philippians 4:6–7 one more time. Keep it handy for every time you face a problem and need to remember where peace comes from. That peace is its own kind of breakthrough.

Let's explore what a good conversation with God looks like in a little more detail.

## TALK TO GOD LIKE A FRIEND

When you're having a conversation with a good friend, how do you speak? Do you use flowery language, repeat yourself, or talk in circles but never really get to the point? Do you guard what you say because you're worried about the impression you're going to make? No, you talk to them in a way that's natural to you, and you trust them to love you, no matter what. That's exactly how we should talk with God.

Unfortunately, we often feel like we need to use lofty language and say everything perfectly when we're praying. But that's just not true. In fact, Jesus wants the opposite from us, as He told us in the Sermon on the Mount in Matthew 6:7–8:

> *When you pray, don't babble on and*
> *on as people of other religions do. They think*
> *their prayers are answered merely by repeating*
> *their words again and again. Don't be like*
> *them, for your Father knows exactly what you*
> *need even before you ask him!*

When you pray, share what's on your heart, honestly. If you're happy, pray happily. If you're upset about something, be upset. It's okay to be transparent with God. He's God. He can handle your emotions. You should feel free to tell Him exactly how you feel. The truth is, He already knows what's in your heart; He just wants you to talk to Him about it.

---

It's okay to be transparent with God.
He's God. He can handle your emotions.

---

Remember that hymn I shared earlier, "What a Friend We Have in Jesus"? Here's the original third verse:

> *Are we weak and heavy laden,*
> *cumbered with a load of care?*
>
> *Precious Savior, still our refuge—*
> *take it to the Lord in prayer!*
>
> *Do your friends despise, forsake you?*
> *Take it to the Lord in prayer!*
>
> *In his arms he'll take and shield you;*
> *you will find a solace there.*[3]

Romans 5:11 reminds us of the great friend we have in God—a friendship Jesus' life, death and resurrection secured for us:

---

3  Joseph Medlicott Scriven, "What a Friend We Have in Jesus."

*So now we can rejoice in our wonderful new
relationship with God because our Lord Jesus
Christ has made us friends of God.*

## BE THANKFUL, EVEN WHEN
## YOU'RE STRUGGLING

When you have a problem, it tends to dominate your
thinking. You may have what my friends and I (C.A.)
jokingly call *swirly brain*. You're thinking about a million things all at once at whiplash speed. Everything
is swirling together in your mind, and there's usually
some major anxiety at the center of it all—the core
problem. When I have swirly brain, I usually start my
conversations with God by launching right into my
problem. Can you relate?

When we start our prayers by laying out our problems, it's easy to develop a complaining spirit. That
complaining spirit keeps us from welcoming in the
fullness of God's comfort. On the other hand, when
we come to God with a grateful heart, we'll be much
more open to receiving what He has ready and waiting for us—Himself. He's what we need most. So, as
the phrase goes, *count your blessings*!

I've learned this lesson through personal experience. As I (Nelson) was deep in my cancer battle, I
formed friendships with other men of a similar age

going through similar hardships. I call them my chemo buddies. One was a deacon—an appointed helper to his church and the church's pastors—so we had a lot in common through our faith. We would often schedule our all-day treatments on the same day so we had a lot of time to talk when we felt like it.

Our conversation usually started with an Organ Recital, which is not what you think; it has nothing to do with music. In our Organ Recital, we would talk through the status of our organs, reciting how cancer was impacting them, the pain we experienced, or the new surgeries we faced.

It felt good to share with another person who could relate to my experience. But after a couple of months' worth of Organ Recitals, my friend suggested that we also begin sharing our blessings—good things, not just the bad stuff.

In my mind, I objected immediately: *Look, I'm the godliest of the two of us. I have the theological degrees and ministry experience, so if anyone is going to take our conversation in a spiritual direction, it's going to be me!* But God quickly humbled me. I let my holier-than-though attitude drop and suggested he start.

He thought for a moment, then said, "Well, I can still pee standing up!"

We both doubled over laughing, almost pulling our chemo needles from their ports. The nurse even came down to check on us. It became a running joke between us, a joke only two guys enduring chemo on the borderline of a health breakdown could appreciate. (I hope you aren't too offended.)

After that, we added a Grateful List to our Organ Recital every time we were together. Despite our problems, we had a lot to be grateful for, like our faith, families and friendship. The Organ Recital was helpful for sure, but the Grateful List was life-changing because when we shared it, we did it knowing it was an offering to God.

The apostle Paul wrote to the church in Thessalonica in 1 Thessalonians 5:18, "Be thankful in all circumstances, for this is God's will for you who belong to Christ Jesus." Note that Paul didn't say give thanks *for* all circumstances; he said to give thanks *in* all circumstances. There's a difference. You don't have to be thankful for the problem—some struggles are so painful you would scoff at the idea of being grateful for them—but Paul was saying to be thankful in the midst of all things, no matter how hopeless they may seem.

Take it from me: Something incredible happens when you begin talking with God by first saying thank you. Even when you don't feel it, when you start a prayer saying, "God, first let me say thank you for my salvation. Thank you for my family, my friends, my church, my job, my health," you will begin to see you have far more blessings than you have problems.

## BE PERSISTENT IN
## TALKING WITH GOD

When you were a kid, how often did you pester your parents for something you wanted? Probably quite often! Kids are naturally good at asking for what they want or need over and over and over again. In Scripture, God encourages us to pray in a similar way—to come to Him again and again for our everyday wants and needs. Persistence in prayer is the key to unlocking God's heart. As Jesus told us:

> *Keep on asking, and you will receive what*
> *you ask for. Keep on seeking, and you will*
> *find. Keep on knocking, and the door will*
> *be opened to you. For everyone who asks,*
> *receives. Everyone who seeks, finds. And to*
> *everyone who knocks, the door will be opened.*
> (Matthew 7:7–8)

But why? If the answer is no, why doesn't He just say no? And if the answer is yes, why doesn't He give us what we're asking for and be done with it? Why does He want us to keep on asking?

First, persistence in prayer draws you closer to God. Think about the voices of those closest to you. When you hear the voice of someone you talk to often—someone you are in close relationship with—you can recognize it immediately. Similarly, the more you talk with God, the more you're going to be able to recognize His voice when He speaks.

If you don't spend time talking with God, you could miss His voice when He tries to communicate with you. He may try to talk to you through different aspects of your life, and you may not recognize His voice because you haven't spent enough time with Him for it to be familiar. God wants you to pray persistently because, in that communication, there's something bigger going on than having your prayer answered. You're getting to know Him better.

---

If you don't spend time talking
with God, you could miss His voice when
He tries to communicate with you.

---

Second, persistence in prayer grows your faith. It makes you more like Jesus. You see, prayer doesn't bend God's will to ours. Prayer bends our will to God's. When we talk to God, it transforms our perspective. We begin to see our circumstances with fresh eyes, and most importantly, our faith grows. Sometimes, what we're asking for isn't God's best for us, and as we talk to God and share what's on our heart, letting Him know what we want—which we should, even if it's not His will for us—He shapes and changes our heart to be like His. He transforms us to want His best for us. It's a miracle, really. When we're persistent in praying, we grow closer to God. In the process, we're shaped to be more like Him and to see the world as He does.

## BE READY TO OBEY WHAT GOD TELLS YOU

One reason we avoid talking to God about our problems is that sometimes we're afraid of what He's going to say. Even though God's way is always the best way, it's seldom the easiest way—and it's rarely the path everyone else is taking (see Matthew 7:13).

So, when we're talking to God about something difficult, we must remember that He loves us more than we can imagine. His will for us is far better than our own. He desires us to be able to trust Him enough to say, "God, whatever you tell me to do, my answer is yes." That's the kind of faith Jesus demonstrated for us on earth.

Are you in the middle of a struggle right now? Have you been resisting talking to God about it? Let me encourage you to stop reading and spend a moment in prayer. Talk to Him like a friend. Tell Him how thankful you are for His presence in your life. Be honest about what's going on in your heart. Give your struggle over to Him. Ask Him to bring a breakthrough.

Tomorrow, do the same thing. And the next day. And the next day. Be persistent, and as you pray, whatever God tells you to do, be ready to do it.

In John 10:27, Jesus says, "My sheep listen to my voice; I know them, and they follow me." When you're praying with thankfulness, unburdening your heart, and lifting everything up to Him, instead of saying, "Amen," try saying, "Okay, God. I'm listening." Then listen. Be still and quiet in His presence.

Now, more than likely, God is not going to speak to you in an audible voice, but He will speak to your heart. He will speak through His Word as you read Scripture. He'll speak to you through the Holy Spirit comforting you, counseling you, convicting you and guiding you in the right direction.

Ask yourself, *Is there something I know God has been telling me to do, but I haven't done it?* Maybe you're afraid it'll be hard. You're not confident about what's going to happen. Perhaps you just don't want to do it.

Doing whatever God is telling you to do may indeed mean that some difficult changes need to occur.

Maybe some habits need to be broken.

Maybe some relationships need to be mended.

Maybe some attitudes need to shift.

And in all of that, your faith is going to have to overcome any fear. Whatever God is telling you to do, trust Him and follow. He is the God who loves you. He is the God who beckons you. He is the God of every breakthrough.

(For more on prayer, including a free download of a multi-part teaching on the Lord's Prayer, which ties in directly with the principles from this book, see www.Breakthrough-Book.com.)

# GOD'S POWER IN A PROBLEM

## *Jesus Raises a Widow's Son*
### Luke 7:11–17

Soon afterward Jesus went with his disciples to the village of Nain, and a large crowd followed him. A funeral procession was coming out as he approached the village gate. The young man who had died was a widow's only son, and a large crowd from the village was with her. When the Lord saw her, his heart over-flowed with compassion. "Don't cry!" he said. Then he walked over to the coffin and touched it, and the bearers stopped. "Young man," he said, "I tell you, get up." Then the dead boy sat up and began to talk! And Jesus gave him back to his mother.

Great fear swept the crowd, and they praised God, saying, "A mighty prophet has risen among us," and "God has visited his people today." And the news about Jesus spread throughout Judea and the sur-rounding countryside.

## CHAPTER 3

# KEEPING YOUR PROBLEMS IN PERSPECTIVE

For many of us, one unexpected bill makes us leap to thoughts of impending bankruptcy. One roof leak convinces us our home is about to fall in. One breakup has us feeling like we'll never find love again. In other words, we tend to exaggerate our problems.

A propensity to make things worse than they really are is part of our human nature. Psychologists even have a name for it: *magnification*. We often magnify even our small problems, turning them into larger problems that overwhelm us and keep us from maintaining a proper godly perspective.

It's like we steep ourselves in a fog that makes it hard to see clearly. The military has a name for this too: *the fog of war*. The *fog of war* refers to being locked in a battle but unable to see the whole picture. You don't know the details of your situation—where the enemy is, how many of them there are, or what kind of weapons they have—so you end up having to make your decisions in a fog, of sorts. The story of Gideon in the book of Judges is an excellent example of operating under the fog of war.

Gideon, an Israelite, was locked in a battle against 135,000 soldiers from Midian, Israel's enemy. Gideon only had 300 Israelite soldiers. Even so, God told Gideon to take his 300 men and surround the Midianite army's campground in the middle of the night. The Israelite soldiers carried trumpets as well as torches concealed in clay jars. Once they had surrounded the Midianites, they blew the trumpets and busted the jars. That burst of hundreds of flames lit up the night sky, so when the Midianites woke up, they thought a much larger army surrounded them. They were confused, lost in the fog of war. They didn't know who the enemy was, how many of them there were, or exactly where they were, so the Midianites ended up running around killing many of their own.

Decisions made in the fog of war don't often have good outcomes. This is true with military encounters as well as with the problems we face in our own lives. As a pastor, I've noticed that when someone is facing a problem, they often get overwhelmed by a sense of stress. The fog of war skews reality and they panic. Poor decisions, hurt and defeat usually follow.

However, there are some important steps we can take to avoid magnifying our problems and losing ground in the fog of war. When we stay calm and adopt the right mindset, we're better able to invite God's transforming power into our situation and open ourselves to receiving a breakthrough. Remember, God always has a solution to your problem. As you allow the Holy Spirit to guide you toward that solution, the result will be a deeper walk with Jesus. But you must do your part to cooperate with Him by choosing to lean into the godly principles that can help you have the same attitude as Christ. For starters, be intentional about viewing your problems from God's perspective.

---

When we stay calm and adopt
the right mindset, we're better able
to invite God's transforming power into
our situation and open ourselves to
receiving a breakthrough.

---

## VIEW YOUR PROBLEMS FROM GOD'S PERSPECTIVE

No matter how smart or spiritually mature you are, it's hard to see clearly in the fog of war. Imagine you're facing a problem that would register around a level 3 in severity (on a scale of 1 to 10). If you're in the fog of war, you may unwittingly make a wrong decision that suddenly jumps your problem from a level 3 to a level 9.

For example, say you don't get a promotion you think you deserve. That's likely a level 3 problem, but your emotions take over, and you feel like your world is coming to an end. The next day, you go into work with a bitter spirit. Your frustration causes you to make poor decisions that you wouldn't have made the day before. You decide you need to tell your boss exactly how you feel, so you stomp into her office and let her have it. That leads your boss to call her boss, which necessitates a disciplinary meeting for you. A level 3 problem is now a level 8 or 9 problem because, in the fog of your own emotions and limited perspective, you've put your job on the line.

Maybe your family life is getting chaotic and your friends all like to pour out their problems to you. The emotional toll of your family and friend relationships is starting to feel too great. In reality, this may be a level 5 problem for you. You just want to pull back for a while—take a break from people and their issues. But when you start clearing your schedule to do that, the first thing you cut is your small group. Then church attendance goes on the chopping block. Before you know it, you're neglecting your personal time with God. In your attempt to meet your need for some downtime, you've removed the very things that are necessary to give you strength in your difficult relationships. In your fog, a level 5 problem has become a level 10 problem because you've pushed yourself away from what's most important to every area of your well-being.

---

God sees the full picture of every
situation you face.

---

Whether it's a bad grade, an unexpected medical expense, an issue with your kids, or a fight with your spouse, your problems get worse when you're in a fog because you make decisions informed by stress. Thankfully, even when you can't see clearly, God can. His perspective is far wiser and more encompassing than yours.

God sees the full picture of every situation you face. While your problem may seem impossible from your perspective, from God's perspective, not only is there a breakthrough available, but He's also going to use what you're going through to make you more complete in Him. As James wrote:

*Dear brothers and sisters, when troubles of any kind come your way, consider it an opportunity for great joy. For you know that when your faith is tested, your endurance has a chance to grow. So let it grow, for when your endurance is fully developed, you will be perfect and complete, needing nothing.* (James 1:2–4)

Theologian C.S. Lewis' story "Meditation in a Toolshed," from *God in the Dock*, is a brilliant portrait of what it looks like to shift your perspective. It's worth sharing an excerpt here:

*I was standing today in the dark toolshed. The sun was shining outside and through the crack at the top of the door there came a sunbeam. From where I stood that beam of light, with the specks of dust floating in it, was the most striking thing in the place. Everything else was almost pitch-black. I was seeing the beam, not seeing things by it.*

*Then I moved, so that the beam fell on my eyes. Instantly the whole previous picture vanished. I saw no toolshed, and (above all) no beam. Instead I saw, framed in the irregular cranny at the top of the door, green leaves moving on the branches of a tree outside and beyond that, 90 odd million miles away, the sun. Looking along the beam, and looking at the beam are very different experiences.*[4]

The key is to begin to see every problem that comes into your life from God's perspective. Learn to look along the beam rather than at the beam. How? By internalizing these two truths:

- Problems are part of life's journey.

- Problems don't always make sense.

## PROBLEMS ARE PART OF LIFE'S JOURNEY

No one gets through this life problem-free. Yet many mature Christians have bought into the myth that if they believe in Jesus, if they pray a little bit harder,

---

4    C.S. Lewis, "Meditation in a Toolshed," *God in the Dock* (Grand Rapids, Michigan: William B. Eerdmans Publishing Company, 1970), 212.

or if they live a little bit better, God will somehow remove the problems from their life and even prevent new ones from arising. But Jesus never said that. In fact, He said the opposite: "I have told you all this so that you may have peace in me. Here on earth you will have many trials and sorrows. But take heart, because I have overcome the world" (John 16:33).

If you trust God in the face of life's difficulties, He will help you become strong and courageous. He will go before you and never abandon you. As you lean into Him, He will guide you toward the break-through you need. On the other hand, if you buy into the fallacy that a good life equals a problem-free life, you're going to be sorely disappointed. You'll also be tempted to blame someone else when problems rear their head—and that someone else will likely be God.

---

If you trust God in the face of life's difficulties, He will help you become strong and courageous.

---

If you catch yourself thinking that God has forgot-ten you, or that He must not see your pain or hear your cries, watch out. That's the first slippery step toward adopting a wrong perspective on the trials of life. The truth is that problems always have been and always will be part of life's journey. They were even part of Jesus' journey, and He's the Son of God. Understanding the problems Jesus faced makes His words in John 16:33 even more powerful: "But take heart, because I have overcome the world."

That's the perspective we must hold on to. When we reframe our problems to see them through Jesus' eyes, we can have peace knowing the same power that raised Jesus Christ from the dead is available to us, whatever life throws our way. Learning to see your problems from God's perspective moves you from a state of magnification and fog of war to a state of trust, faith and hope that is no longer you-focused but God-focused.

## PROBELMS DON'T ALWAYS MAKE SENSE

Have you ever asked the question *Why is this happening to me?* Or how about *What did I do to deserve this?* We're reasoning people, so we usually want to know the *why* behind the moments that challenge us most. But as difficult as it is to accept, we may never get answers to all our *whys*. Some things God says and allows are simply too big for our limited human understanding. Consider Isaiah 55:8: " 'My thoughts are nothing like your thoughts,' says the LORD. 'And my ways are far beyond anything you could imagine.' "

God's plans are perfect. Even though God may not be causing that problem that keeps discouraging you or beating you down, God—through that problem—is working to bring good out of the bad. He's working to bring order out of confusion, to bring life out of death, and ultimately to mature you in your faith. That's what He does.

---

And when our belief in God grows,
the amount of peace we have grows too.

---

From our limited perspective, we can only see a small part of how God is at work. For many people, that's frustrating and painful; they want to know every detail of His plan, every curve and bend in His path for them. But when we acknowledge that God can see farther down the road than we can, that helps our faith and trust in Him grow. And when our belief in God grows, the amount of peace we have grows too.

I (C.A.) was on a local swim team when I was a kid. I didn't particularly enjoy swimming, and I wasn't anywhere close to being the best on the team, but I liked doing backstroke and went to each swim meet with a yearning for that silky blue ribbon imprinted with a gold *First Place*. I couldn't wait to get to the end of my lane, slam my hand on the pool's terra-cotta edge, and look up at my coach to hear the name of the winner. But I had two problems: my sense of direction while swimming backstroke was terrible, and I constantly got water in my goggles.

This, unfortunately, resulted in me weaving side to side throughout the lane, hitting my arms against the pool's edge, and then, in an overcorrection, on the plastic floating lines marking off the lanes. It got so bad that I started going more slowly for fear of ricocheting off something else. My mom must've noticed this because, at some point in my swimming career, she started walking—in heels, no less—alongside my lane as I swam, shouting my name, directing my path and cheering on my progress. (Yes, I could hear her under the water; she has that kind of pitch.)

I was afraid and stressed out by my problem. I couldn't see, kept hitting things and had little idea of where I was going. But I heard my mom's voice, followed it above the roar of the crowds and found where I needed to be—touching stone at the end of the race. My mom could see what I couldn't see because she wasn't in the fog that I was in. She had a higher, clearer perspective, and I trusted her authority to lead me well.

In the same way, our limited vision in this world isn't good enough to see us faithfully through this life and into the next, but God's unlimited vision is. He has the highest, clearest perspective there is, and He is the authority over it all. Who can we trust more than Him? As Paul wrote in 1 Corinthians 13:12:

> *Now we see things imperfectly,*
> *like puzzling reflections in a mirror,*
> *but then we will see everything with perfect*
> *clarity. All that I know now is partial and*
> *incomplete, but then I will know everything*
> *completely, just as God now knows*
> *me completely.*

You may never understand why you and your spouse can't get pregnant, why your dad walked out on your family, or why that dream job has never materialized. But if you put your faith in Jesus Christ, there will come a time after your life on earth is over when you will stand in God's presence and be able to see everything with God's perspective. What was once shrouded by the fog will be strikingly clear.

## BE WILLING TO ACCEPT WHAT CAN'T BE CHANGED

In the book of Job, we learn Job was a rich man of God. Think of him as a billionaire of today. He had livestock and land. He had a large, healthy family, a lavish home and many servants.

Then one day he lost everything.

Everything.

Not only did he lose his possessions and wealth, but he also lost his family. The losses came fast and without explanation. There was nothing Job could do to turn back time or to fix it. Job 1:21 captures his response to this sudden devastation:

*He said, "I came naked from my*
*mother's womb, and I will be naked*
*when I leave. The LORD gave me what*
*I had, and the LORD has taken it away.*
*Praise the name of the LORD!"*

How could a response like this even be possible? Job had the right perspective. He knew he couldn't change what had happened, so he accepted it. He also knew God is good and worthy to be praised, even in the most difficult moments of life. He didn't know why he had lost everything dear to him or for what ultimate good God was working on his behalf, but he chose to praise the Lord. Rather than panic, he leaned into and accepted God's peace.

As we've seen, God isn't the source of our problems. Because we are broken people living in a broken world, we experience the pain of brokenness—but God is still good. No matter what happens to us, we can trust that He loves us tremendously, He has a plan, and He's using all things for our good, even when it doesn't seem like it. That knowledge gives us the ability to accept the things that can't be changed. As Romans 8:28 says, "And we know that God causes everything to work together for the good of those who love God and are called according to his purpose for them."

---

Because we are broken people living in a broken world, we experience the pain of brokenness—but God is still good.

---

I remember well the shock of the sudden outbreak of COVID-19 in the US in March 2020 and the ensuing global pandemic. I'm sure we all do. Within a few weeks, the world transformed in ways that were entirely out of our control. It took a few weeks, even months, before I finally came to grips with the fact that the pandemic was here to stay for the immediate future. I couldn't fix the fact that toilet paper was in short supply, travel was barred by lockdown, kids were moving to online school, employees were being furloughed and people were very sick—many dying. For control freaks like me, those were hard pills to swallow.

Since I couldn't change what was happening around me, I had to accept it. I, like all of us, had to surrender my fear to God and receive His peace. During that time, I learned anew that, instead of complaining and arguing, I needed to talk to God about it in prayer. When we exercise this habit, it becomes easier for us to praise Him even in our worst moments because He's still good, still loves us and still offers us His peace, which goes beyond understanding in any and every circumstance (Philippians 4:7).

You're probably familiar with the Serenity Prayer:

*God, grant me the serenity to accept the things*
*I cannot change,*
*courage to change the things I can,*
*and the wisdom to know the difference.*

If we face a problem and it's in our ability to fix it, we should do so with God's leading. But if it's something beyond our control, we must trust God enough to accept it.

---

When you're able to look at
your problems from God's perspective,
you'll begin to see possibilities for
growth and change.

---

## CHOOSE TO SEE PROBLEMS AS A PATH FOR SPIRITUAL GROWTH

Your problems can become part of God's plan for your spiritual growth. They grow your faith. They make you more like Jesus. In James 1:2–3, the apostle wrote, "Dear brothers and sisters, when troubles of any kind come your way, consider it an opportunity for great joy. For you know that when your faith is tested, your endurance has a chance to grow."

When you're able to look at your problems from God's perspective, you'll begin to see possibilities for growth and change. You'll see them as opportunities to trust God more, to let Him develop your character, to learn something new and ultimately to become more like Jesus. Remember Paul's words: "For our present troubles are small and won't last very long.

Yet they produce for us a glory that vastly outweighs them and will last forever!" (2 Corinthians 4:17).

The struggle you're in right now may feel suffocating, but the God who is able to do more than we can ask or imagine can take that struggle and make it a catalyst for positive change in your life. God can use anything that happens in your life to grow you spiritually. The key is to trust Him and to believe that He has a path for you. I'm not saying your problems themselves are positive. On the contrary.

Cancer is terrible.

Your broken heart is devastating.

Abuse is incomprehensible.

A parent abandoning a child is tragic.

A financial crisis, flunking out of school, a worldwide pandemic—those are awful things.

But God specializes in bringing good out of bad. He specializes in taking a problem and using it to lead to a positive change in your life. He wants to do that, and He can, if you'll trust Him. God will bring you a breakthrough that's in harmony with His Word—as all biblical breakthroughs are—and deepens your relationship with Him. In fact, there are areas of maturity that you will only experience in your Christian walk because of problems.

When you're in a fog, it's hard to see beyond the present pain, beyond the next few days, weeks, or even months. But God's view isn't related to your weekly calendar; His view includes eternity. So, if you want to see your problems through God's eyes, you've got to realize that He's planning for an eternity in heaven with the perfected *you*.

In the scope of that eternity, you're going to look at the problems you face in this life and realize, joyfully, that they aren't as devastating as they feel right now. If you could see what God already sees about your future, you wouldn't be afraid; you'd have faith. You wouldn't panic; you'd have peace. No wonder the Bible constantly challenges us to keep eternity in mind—it gives us the right perspective for receiving God's breakthrough.

# GOD'S POWER IN A PROBLEM

## *Paul and Silas in Prison*
Acts 16:25–34

Around midnight Paul and Silas were praying and singing hymns to God, and the other prisoners were listening. Suddenly, there was a massive earthquake, and the prison was shaken to its foundations. All the doors immediately flew open, and the chains of every prisoner fell off! The jailer woke up to see the prison doors wide open. He assumed the prisoners had escaped, so he drew his sword to kill himself. But Paul shouted to him, "Stop! Don't kill yourself! We are all here!"

The jailer called for lights and ran to the dungeon and fell down trembling before Paul and Silas. Then he brought them out and asked, "Sirs, what must I do to be saved?"

They replied, "Believe in the Lord Jesus and you will be saved, along with everyone in your household." And they shared the word of the Lord with him and with all who lived in his household. Even at that hour of the night, the jailer cared for them and washed their wounds. Then he and everyone in his household were immediately baptized. He brought them into his house and set a meal before them, and he and his entire household rejoiced because they all believed in God.

CHAPTER 4

# KNOWING GOD'S PEACE

For years, researchers have been studying the physiological effects of problem-related stress on our bodies. According to their findings, when we're facing difficult situations, we breathe faster to get more oxygen into our lungs. Our heart beats faster, and our blood pressure rises. We don't feel injuries as acutely because our pain receptors dial down. Our mouth gets dry. Our throat tightens. We start to sweat. Our hair even stands on end.

These involuntary responses don't seem to leave much room for peace, do they? No, peace is not a normal physiological reaction when we are under stress. Panic is. Fear is. But peace? That doesn't come naturally. If we're going to have peace in the face of problems, it must come from somewhere higher than ourselves.

There's a common misconception that all our problems need to be solved before we can be peaceful and happy, but that's not going to happen on this side of heaven. Think back to Jesus' words:

> *I have told you all this so that you*
> *may have peace in me. Here on earth you*
> *will have many trials and sorrows. But take*
> *heart, because I have overcome the world.*
> (John 16:33)

We are to take heart *during* the trials we face on earth. There are always going to be problems we just can't fix, but those of us who believe in Jesus Christ can have peace amidst any crisis. And not just temporary, distract-from-the-problem peace, but real, deep, unwavering peace—the kind we can't create or maintain on our own. This peace is a supernatural gift that comes from Jesus to those who trust Him, no matter the issues they're facing. Jesus also said:

> *I am leaving you with a gift—*
> *peace of mind and heart. And the peace*
> *I give is a gift the world cannot give.*
> *So don't be troubled or afraid.*
> (John 14:27)

So how do we receive His peace? The first step is to acknowledge that He is in control.

## ACKNOWLEDGE THAT GOD IS IN CONTROL

Sometimes when we're facing problems, it feels like life is spinning in uncontrollable directions, doesn't it? We may be doing our best to control our circumstances and the people around us, but at some point, we realize we can't. We begin to think, *God, don't you see what's going on in my life? Don't you care? Don't you know how I'm feeling?*

He does see you. He does know what you're going through. He knows how you're feeling. And no matter how chaotic your life may seem, He is in full control. Colossians 1:16 reminds us of that:

> *Through him God created everything in the heavenly realms and on earth. He made the things we can see and the things we can't see—such as thrones, kingdoms, rulers, and authorities in the unseen world. Everything was created through him and for him.*

Everything. God created everything in the heavenly realms and on earth. He made the things we can see and the things we can't. Everything was created through Him and for Him. He knows everything that's going on with you. He knows what you've been through, and maybe more importantly, He knows what's still coming down the pike. Your problems don't surprise Him, and He's not at a loss for a solution to them. He is in complete control. Full stop. When your relationships feel strained, when your job is taking a toll on your spiritual life, when your kids are rebelling, when your financial future is falling apart, God is in control.

On the day I received my stage 4 cancer diagnosis, I could not have been more surprised. My doctors were surprised too. Just months earlier, I had completed an executive physical, which is a fancy term for an intensive physical exam. All my numbers were good. The only suggestion I was given was to add a vitamin D pill to my routine. At the same time, I was at a good weight for my stature, and my exercise plan was continuing to improve. I was even preparing for my first 10K run. All signs pointed to health…until they didn't.

Upon my diagnosis, I began meeting with a series of doctors. They all asked about family history of cancer (none!) and if I had any symptoms related to my type of cancer. I'd had a flu-like fever and an upset stomach that I considered a small bug about a month before the cancer was discovered, but nothing that made it seem more than just a natural consequence of a heavy travel schedule. It seemed like the kind of mild sickness we've all experienced. I'd had no symptoms that would chart as indicative of serious disease.

I share all of this to underscore that I could not have been more shocked to receive my cancer diagnosis. My wife and family were all dumbfounded as well. But it's not unusual for us to be surprised by problems, is it? In fact, looking back, almost all the problems I've faced came as a surprise. I bet you could say the same. It's the unexpected nature of problems that make them so challenging.

The problems you're facing right now may be a surprise to you, but they are not a surprise to God. Your problems may rock you, but they don't rock God. You may be at a loss for a solution, but God isn't. God is in control when you don't know what to do. God is in control when you can't see the road ahead and are afraid for your future. He's *in control.*

---

The problems you're facing right
now may be a surprise to you, but they
are not a surprise to God.

---

To find peace during your problem, you must acknowledge that reality, even when it feels like your life is spinning out of control. You'll only be able to rest in God's peace when you can say, "God, I know that you're God and I'm not. No matter how much I want to control the situation, no matter how much I want to be able to move things around, I can't. Only You can. So I'm going to rest in the knowledge that You're in control. You've got this. You've got me." There is a God and you're not Him. Neither am I. When we acknowledge that, we can lean into His ways and His peace.

When we look back, we can see how God has been faithful to walk with us through life's ups and downs in the past. Remembering what we've been brought through helps us have peace in the present, accepting what we can't control and trusting that God is good. Psalm 77:11 says it this way: "But then I recall all you have done, O LORD; I remember your wonderful deeds of long ago."

There's an old hymn that speaks so aptly to the peace we can have when we remember God's faithfulness. A devout Christian named Horatio Spafford wrote "It Is Well with My Soul" in the 19th century. Horatio was a successful lawyer in Chicago with a beautiful family, but in 1871, he and his wife endured the tragic loss of their son. Just a few months later, the Great Chicago Fire occurred, and the Spaffords lost almost everything. Two years after that, Horatio put his wife and four daughters on a Europe-bound boat for a vacation, but there was a collision, and all four of his daughters drowned, his wife the only survivor. In the middle of the Atlantic on a boat to England to meet his grieving wife and bury their four daughters, Horatio penned these words:

*When peace like a river attendeth my way,*
*When sorrows like sea-billows roll,*
*Whatever my lot Thou hast taught me to know;*
*It is well, it is well with my soul.*

How is it possible that Horatio could write such a thing? Only God knows, considering it was only possible through Him. And for our inspiration, here's the rest of the hymn. Let these words speak to your soul:

*Tho' Satan should buffet, tho' trials should come,*
*Let this blest assurance control,*
*That Christ hath regarded my helpless estate,*
*And hath shed his own blood for my soul.*

*My sin—oh, the bliss of this glorious thought!*
*My sin—not in part but the whole,*
*Is nailed to His cross and I bear it no more;*
*Praise the Lord, praise the Lord, oh my soul!*

*And, Lord, haste the day when the faith shall be sight,*
*The clouds be rolled back as a scroll,*

*The trump shall resound, and the Lord shall descend*
*A song in the night, oh my soul!*

*For me, be it Christ, be it Christ hence to live,*
*If Jordan above me shall roll,*
*No pang shall be mine, for in death as in life*
*Thou wilt whisper Thy peace to my soul.*

*It is well with my soul,*
*It is well, it is well with my soul.*[5]

## PRACTICE BLESSING OTHERS

The second way to experience God's peace in the face of hardship is to shift our attention away from ourselves and onto someone else. When we're wading through difficult issues in our own lives, we tend to get incredibly self-focused. We become so zeroed in on what we need that we forget there are others around us who need help too. It's during these times that blessing others can bless us more than we realize. Consider Paul's words to a group of church elders:

*And I have been a constant example*
*of how you can help those in need by working*
*hard. You should remember the words of the*

---

5    Horatio Spafford, "It Is Well with My Soul," 1873, SpaffordHymn.com.

*Lord Jesus, "It is more blessed to give,
than it is to receive." (Acts 20:35)*

When we're in trouble, desperate for healing and peace and purpose, the best thing we can do is follow Jesus' example and take His words to heart. "It is more blessed to give than to receive." But often, we're too busy letting our own problems control us to help others. We're busy obsessing over our own stuff, getting angry and feeling overwhelmed. Instead of thinking about serving others, we serve our pain, which just keeps it alive.

---

When we're in trouble, desperate
for healing and peace and purpose,
the best thing we can do is follow Jesus'
example and take His words to heart. "It is
more blessed to give than to receive."

---

If we can break out of that and begin to bless others amid our own pain, something supernatural happens: We receive real peace, Jesus' peace. With His peace, we begin to experience His joy. And even though our problem may not be fixed, we suddenly have a different perspective on it, on how God is working in our lives and in the lives of those around us.

When I was deep into my chemotherapy treatment and feeling crummy, my doctor came to me one day with a question. He told me about a man my age with a similar condition who was about to start chemo and asked if he could assign him the chair next to mine. My doctor thought, if the opportunity presented itself, I might encourage this man and talk him through what to expect since I was a bit further down the road than him. He said he wanted my *positive attitude* to rub off on the guy.

I was surprised. Up until this point, I was too focused on my treatment to consider who was in the chair beside me. And I felt guilty that a good, moral, but non-Christian doctor was the person God was using to break me out of my self-centeredness. About three hours into the chemo, a conversational door opened, and I did all I could to encourage my new chemo buddy (yes, that's how we referred to each other, and we still do). As I left treatment that day, I felt nauseated like usual, but I also felt, well, blessed—*profoundly* blessed by how God had forced me outside of my problem to help someone else with theirs. As Proverbs 11:25 says, "The generous will prosper; those who refresh others will themselves be refreshed."

When we're facing a problem and we need peace, we should stop and look around at the people God has placed in our lives and ask ourselves, *How can I be a blessing to them? How can I serve them?* Then let's do it and watch Him work through our efforts.

(In my book *The Greatness Principle: Finding Significance through Service*, I teach this powerful principle: God blesses you when you bless others. Part of your breakthrough may come when you bless others by serving them. For more, see www.Breakthrough-Book.com.)

## KEEP ETERNITY IN MIND

We have all heard someone describe a beautiful place as *heaven on earth*. And it's true there are times while we're on earth that we get small glimpses of the place Jesus is readying for us in eternity (John 14:1–4). But the heavenly feeling we experience from a beautiful vista or a great vacation is always short-lived. We're plunged back to reality by bills, arguments, stomach bugs and stress. Our problems remind us that earth is earth; it is not heaven. But for all who have placed their faith in Jesus, heaven is coming.

No matter how we might try, we'll never be able to turn our imperfect earthly experience into something resembling heaven, but thanks to Jesus, Christians have an eternity of perfection to look forward to—an eternity of complete peace, joy and love free from sin and stress. In Revelation 21:3–4, the apostle John wrote:

> *I heard a loud shout from the throne, saying,*
> *"Look, God's home is now among his people!*
> *He will live with them, and they will be his*
> *people. God himself will be with them. He will*
> *wipe every tear from their eyes, and there will*
> *be no more death or sorrow or crying or pain.*
> *All these things are gone forever."*

We can rest in God's peace during our earthly trials by keeping our focus on the perfection that is to come.

Even nonbelievers feel a pull toward heaven in their hearts. As the old saying goes, *there are no atheists in foxholes*. We long for God and an eternity spent with Him. We all know deep down that we were created for more than this life.

---

We can rest in God's peace during
our earthly trials by keeping our focus
on the perfection that is to come.

---

The Bible is clear that eternity can be spent in one of two ways. One is an eternity spent in the presence of God, His love and His peace in heaven. The other is an eternity separated from God, away from His peace, in a place the Bible calls hell. But contrary to what many people believe, God doesn't choose where you're going to spend eternity—you do. As C.S. Lewis once wrote:

> *There are only two kinds of people in the end: those who say to God, "Thy will be done," and those to whom God says, in the end, "Thy will be done." All that are in Hell, choose it. Without that self-choice there could be no Hell. No soul that seriously and constantly desires joy will ever miss it.*[6]

As you think about eternity, what stirs in your spirit? Peace? Fear? I hope this discussion has prompted some serious self-reflection. The most important questions I can ask you are these: Have you put your faith in Jesus? Have you trusted in Jesus' death on the cross as the payment for your sins and asked Him to be the Lord of your life? If not, why wait any longer? I encourage you to surrender everything you are and

---

6    C.S. Lewis, *The Great Divorce* (London: Geoffrey Bles, 1945), 72.

everything you have to God and ask Jesus to be your Savior today.

Not only can Jesus offer us the breakthrough for all the pain and suffering we face on a regular basis, but He is our ultimate breakthrough incarnate. He came to this earth to provide the solution for the ultimate problem—our sin and separation from God. He did this to reconcile us to God the Father and draw us into a deeper walk with Him. He is the perfect embodiment of every breakthrough we'll ever need.

# GOD'S POWER IN A PROBLEM

### *Water from the Rock*
Exodus 17:1–6

At the LORD's command, the whole community of Israel left the wilderness of Sin and moved from place to place. Eventually they camped at Rephidim, but there was no water there for the people to drink. So once more the people complained against Moses. "Give us water to drink!" they demanded.

"Quiet!" Moses replied. "Why are you complaining against me? And why are you testing the LORD?"

But tormented by thirst, they continued to argue with Moses. "Why did you bring us out of Egypt? Are you trying to kill us, our children, and our livestock with thirst?"

Then Moses cried out to the LORD, "What should I do with these people? They are ready to stone me!"

The LORD said to Moses, "Walk out in front of the people. Take your staff, the one you used when you struck the water of the Nile, and call some of the elders of Israel to join you. I will stand before you on the rock at Mount Sinai. Strike the rock, and water will come gushing out. Then the people will be able to drink." So Moses struck the rock as he was told, and water gushed out as the elders looked on.

CHAPTER 5

# GOD, THE PROMISE KEEPER

G od's Word is full of promises. In fact, there are over 7,000 promises in the Bible. And the incredible thing is, God keeps every single one of them. God is the consummate promise keeper.

One of the best-known promises in the Old Testament is one God made to an elderly couple named Abraham and Sarah. Abraham and Sarah had been trying to have a baby for decades, but they couldn't. Time had passed and they'd grown very old. At the time of this story, Abraham was 99, and his wife, Sarah, 90. It seemed too late for them to conceive. But God showed up and changed things. One day, God came to Abraham and told him that he and Sarah would have a baby the following year. Genesis 18:11 picks up this story:

> *Abraham and Sarah were both very*
> *old by this time, and Sarah was long past*
> *the age of having children... Then the LORD*
> *said to Abraham,... "Is anything too hard*
> *for the LORD?" (vv. 11, 13, 14)*

We should be asking ourselves that question every time we face a problem: *Is anything too hard for the LORD? Is there any problem I'm facing in my life right now that's too hard for God?* Then God continued, saying:

> *I will return about this time next year, and*
> *Sarah will have a son....For Abraham*
> *will certainly become a great and mighty*
> *nation....I have singled him out so that he*
> *will direct his sons and their families to keep*
> *the way of the LORD by doing what is right*
> *and just. Then I will do for Abraham all that I*
> *have promised. (Genesis 18:14, 18–19)*

It sounded crazy, but Abraham believed God's promise. He knew that God, his Maker, was bigger than the problem of infertility—and even bigger than the reality of old age—and that when God makes a promise, He fulfills it.

And that's exactly what God did. One year later, Isaac was born to Abraham and Sarah. What would come from Isaac was a mighty nation indeed—the nation of Israel.

Abraham and Sarah knew what it meant to wait on God. A little backstory: When God came to tell Abraham, at 99, that he and Sarah would have a baby, that wasn't the first time God had made this promise to Abraham. Twenty-five years earlier, when Abraham was 75 years old, God had made the same promise. Why did God wait 25 years to fulfill His promise? He wanted to know that Abraham was going to trust Him and hold on to faith that He would keep His promise. And Abraham did. Romans 4:20–21 says Abraham never wavered in believing God's promise. His faith only grew stronger, and in this, he brought glory to God, as he was fully convinced that God keeps His promises.

---

Your view of God will determine
how you approach your problems
when they surface.

---

Do you see God as a promise keeper? Your view of God will determine how you approach your problems when they surface. If you view God as the promise keeper that He is, you will have the courage to trust

Him even when things around you look impossible. But sometimes, when you're stuck in the mire, it's hard to trust the promises that you don't see coming true, isn't it? When you're tempted to doubt whether God will keep His promises to you, be intentional about doing these three things to help you remember that He is the ultimate promise keeper:

- Hold on to God's promises.

- Meditate on God's promises.

- Lean on people who believe God's promises.

## HOLD ON TO GOD'S PROMISES

We live in a culture of immediacy, and most of us have been spoiled by it. When we decide we want or need something, we want it *now*.

We want our online purchase delivered today.

We want the person in front of us to drive faster.

We want the line we're waiting in to move quicker.

But this desire for immediacy often conflicts with the nature of God. He isn't all about the now in the same way we are. And He doesn't work on our time-table. When it comes to God's promises, waiting is often an integral part of the equation.

Sometimes, God is growing us through a problem, and that takes time. It takes time for us to build endurance to have the kind of faith God requires of us to do His work in the world. Other times, God delays His promises because of sin and disobedience in our lives. Until we acknowledge, confess, turn our sin over to God and say, "Father, I don't want to do that anymore. I want to surrender this to You. I want to follow after You," God waits. He wants us to learn to trust Him. If God gave us everything we wanted every time we asked for it, as soon as we asked for it, we'd be even more spoiled than we already are today—and likely ignorant of our daily need for His presence and mercy. So we must wait on Him and His promises. We must *hold on*.

That phrase—*hold on*—is something commonly said, a kind of hand-on-shoulder, friendly assurance. When you're going through something difficult in life, friends may say something like "Just hold on. You'll get through it." But what no one seems to ask (because it's likely none of us knows the answer) is, "Hold on to what?"

Whatever we're holding on to, it should be strong—stronger than we are. It should be secure, trustworthy, unfailing. Something that anchors us in place when the storm roars around us. As Jesus said:

*Anyone who listens to my teaching and follows it is wise, like a person who builds a house on solid rock. Though the rain comes in torrents and the floodwaters rise and the winds beat against that house, it won't collapse because it is built on bedrock. But anyone who hears my teaching and doesn't obey it is foolish, like a person who builds a house on sand. When the rains and floods come and the winds beat against that house, it will collapse with a mighty crash.* (Matthew 7:24–27)

Many people try to build their houses on good feelings. To lessen the pain of their situation in life, they say, "I'm just going to do what feels right, or what makes me feel happy right now." But what we feel is right isn't always actually right since our feelings can be deceptive. As Jeremiah 17:9 says, "The human heart is the most deceitful of all things."

---

Whatever we're holding on to,
it should be strong—stronger than we are.
It should be secure, trustworthy, unfailing.
Something that anchors us in place when
the storm roars around us.

---

Other people hold on to a grudge when they go through a problem. They tell themselves, *If I can get through this storm, then I'm going to let that person have it. I'm going to get revenge.* But anger is draining, foolish and dangerous. A house cannot stand on anger when the rains and floods come.

What we hold on to needs to be strong and sure. More so, it needs to be eternal. Only God checks all those boxes. God is our rock. Not only can we trust in His promises to get us through hardship, but we can also trust that His words are strong enough to hold us even in the middle of it.

About six months into the COVID-19 pandemic, I asked some people in my community how they were doing. They shared their heartbreak over the global situation, but many also shared that the pandemic had given them more time to pray, that they started meeting with God in nature, or that they had signed up for online spiritual growth classes. Maybe they told me those things because they know I'm a person of faith, but I felt it was deeper than that. These folks, most of whom would not identify as Christians, found that their problems drew them closer to God. When they leaned into Him, they found that He was sure, steady and trustworthy. So they began looking at what was eternal—began holding on to the character of God— instead of succumbing to the instability around them.

When we learn how to hold on to God during our storms, we can draw strength from His promises to us. As Psalm 119:50 says, "Your promise revives me; it comforts me in all my troubles." (For more on facing life's toughest storms with strength, see my book *Unshakable: Standing Strong When Things Go Wrong*.)

---

What if we were to stop meditating on life's problems and instead begin to meditate on God's promises?

---

## MEDITATE ON GOD'S PROMISES

The concept of meditation gets a bad rap in Christian circles. While the Bible never promotes an empty-minded approach to meditation, it does use the word *meditate* (and similar variations) 29 times to refer to how a believer should handle God's Word and God's promises. Scripture tells us to meditate on God's promises, as in, we should spend quiet time thinking deeply about or focusing our mind on God's Word.

Whether you realize it or not, you probably meditate all the time—on something. The problem is, we don't tend to meditate on God's promises. Instead, we meditate on life's issues. We allow them to dominate our thoughts. We ruminate on them. We worry. We worry to the point that worry becomes a habit. When worry habitually fills our mind, we are, in essence, meditating on our problems.

What if we were to stop meditating on life's problems and instead begin to meditate on God's promises? What a difference that would make in our lives! Psalm 119:15–16 says, "I will study your commandments and reflect on your ways. I will delight in your decrees and not forget your word."

- We're to *study* God's Word. To learn what the meaning is.

- We're to *reflect on* God's Word. To let its meaning sink in, change us and transform us.

- We're to *delight in* God's Word. To take great pleasure in the words God has shared.

- We're to *memorize* God's Word. To store His words in our hearts and minds. (See Appendix B for a key verse to memorize based on each breakthrough principle from this book; it's a good place to start in your Scripture memory journey.)

When God brings us a breakthrough, it will always be a solution that is in harmony with His Word, so we would be wise to be intentional about knowing His Word as well as we can.

Recently, a mentor of mine (C.A.) gave me the idea to write Bible verses down on blank note cards to carry around with me in an attempt to memorize more Scripture. She called these note cards my *stones of David,* tucked away for the darker moments in life when I'm facing a Goliath-sized fear or temptation. Taking the idea one step further, I've begun to tape them in places around my home so I see God's promises wherever I look.

In front of my closet, I put Matthew 6:19: "Don't store up treasures here on earth, where moths eat them and rust destroys them, and where thieves break in and steal."

On the door of my bedroom, so I'll see it when I leave for the day, is 1 Thessalonians 5:16–18: "Always be joyful. Never stop praying. Be thankful in all circumstances, for this is God's will for you who belong to Christ Jesus."

I find it helpful to tape these verses to a specific place where I'm performing a particular action so that when the time comes to act, the words will ring as a clear bell in my mind, helping me to make the godly choice. However, while we're studying, reflecting on and delighting in God's Word, we shouldn't stop there. We're called to *do it*, as James 1:22 says: "But don't just listen to God's word. You must do what it says. Otherwise, you are only fooling yourselves."

If you struggle with memorization, try praying God's Word. Something like this: "Dear God, just like Romans 8:39 says, I believe that You're with me, that nothing will ever separate me from Your love. God, thank You that even though I feel alone right now, I know that I'm not."

Or "Dear Heavenly Father, just like Philippians 4:13 says, I can do everything through Christ who gives me strength, so help me remember that tomorrow as I go into my job interview, which is causing me so much anxiety."

Whatever you're facing, be intentional about meditating on God's promises. You can trust Him to keep His word.

## LEAN ON PEOPLE WHO BELIEVE GOD'S PROMISES

When you have a problem, everybody has an opinion, don't they? Your mom has an opinion. Your best friend has an opinion. The guy at the coffee shop has an opinion. But not everybody's opinion should influence you. The opinions that do matter in your life are those of godly people, those who are truly walking with the Father. Godly people want God's best in your life. They will point you to Him and His Word when you're struggling. As Proverbs 13:20 says, "Walk with the wise and become wise; associate with fools and get in trouble."

You wouldn't ask a drunk person at a bar how to stop drinking; that doesn't make any sense. You wouldn't ask someone who's been divorced three times to tell you the secrets to a lifelong marriage; they're probably not going to have a lot of good advice for you. You wouldn't ask the guy who just got fired from another job how to have a successful career; asking him probably wouldn't even occur to you.

---

The brothers and sisters in Christ
we take the time to nurture relationships
with are the people who will point us back
to the promises of God.

---

Ultimately, God's opinion is the only one that matters, but one of the primary ways God speaks into our lives is through His people. We desperately need people in our lives who will remind us of His character, who are willing to say, when we're about to make a foolish decision, "Hey, are you sure you want to do that? Let's pray about it first." This is what Galatians 6:2 calls us to: "Share each other's burdens, and in this way obey the law of Christ."

Surrounding yourself with godly people who can share your burdens and advise you with wisdom is part of why attending church is so important. It's why getting into a Bible study group that prays together is so important. We're not meant to walk through our issues alone. The brothers and sisters in Christ we take the time to nurture relationships with are the people who will point us back to the promises of God.

Yet even when people fail us—as they sometimes do—God's promises remain. Just think of the Israelites. Deuteronomy 31:6 captures a promise God made to the nation of Israel: "So be strong and courageous. Do not be afraid and do not panic before them. For the LORD your God will personally go ahead of you. He will neither fail you nor abandon you."

When God made this promise, the Israelites were facing a major problem. They had finally reached the moment of entering the promised land, but their leader of 40 years, Moses, was not going into the land with them. Worse, he was about to die. They were terrified to be without their leader and in foreign territory, even though God had designated the land as their own. This was when God made His promise to them in Deuteronomy 31:6, that if they would trust Him, He would go ahead of them. He would pave the way.

The same promise that God made to the Israelites all those years ago, God makes to us today if we believe in Him and entrust our lives to Him. Again, there are thousands of promises in the Bible. Here are just a few for you to begin taking to heart. I encourage you to look each one up. Then, as mentioned earlier, consider writing the verses you'd like to meditate over on index cards. Keep them in front of you, and remember to trust God to keep all His promises as you ask Him to guide you toward your breakthrough.

## KEY SCRIPTURE PROMISES FOR BREAKTHROUGH

- **Guidance:**

  For that is what God is like. He is our God forever and ever, and he will guide us until we die. (Psalm 48:14)

  Take delight in the LORD, and he will give you your heart's desires. (Psalm 37:4)

  For I hold you by your right hand—I, the LORD your God. And I say to you, "Don't be afraid. I am here to help you." (Isaiah 41:13)

Seek his will in all you do, and he will show you which path to take. (Proverbs 3:6)

The LORD says, "I will guide you along the best pathway for your life. I will advise you and watch over you." (Psalm 32:8)

- **Wisdom:**
  For the LORD grants wisdom! From his mouth come knowledge and understanding. He grants a treasure of common sense to the honest. He is a shield to those who walk with integrity. (Proverbs 2:6–7)

  If you need wisdom, ask our generous God, and he will give it to you. He will not rebuke you for asking. (James 1:5)

- **Peace:**
  I am leaving you with a gift—peace of mind and heart. And the peace I give is a gift the world cannot give. So don't be troubled or afraid. (John 14:27)

  Therefore, since we have been made right in God's sight by faith, we have peace with God because of what Jesus Christ our Lord has done for us. (Romans 5:1)

  Don't worry about anything; instead, pray about everything. Tell God what you need, and thank him for all he has done. Then you will experience God's peace, which exceeds anything we can understand. His peace will guard your hearts and minds as you live in Christ Jesus. (Philippians 4:6–7)

- **Strength:**
He gives power to the weak and strength to the powerless. Even youths will become weak and tired, and young men will fall in exhaustion. But those who trust in the LORD will find new strength. They will soar high on wings like eagles. They will run and not grow weary. They will walk and not faint. (Isaiah 40:29–31)

Don't be afraid, for I am with you. Don't be discouraged, for I am your God. I will strengthen you and help you. I will hold you up with my victorious right hand. (Isaiah 41:10)

For I can do everything through Christ, who gives me strength. (Philippians 4:13)

- **Provision:**
Seek the Kingdom of God above all else, and live righteously, and he will give you everything you need. (Matthew 6:33)

So if you sinful people know how to give good gifts to your children, how much more will your heavenly Father give good gifts to those who ask him. (Matthew 7:11)

Then, turning to his disciples, Jesus said, "That is why I tell you not to worry about everyday life—whether you have enough food to eat or enough clothes to wear. For life is more than food, and your body more than clothing. Look at the ravens. They don't plant or harvest or store food in barns, for God feeds them. And you are far more valuable to him than any birds!" (Luke 12:22–24)

And this same God who takes care of me will supply all your needs from his glorious riches, which have been given to us in Christ Jesus. (Philippians 4:19)

- **Healing:**
Such a prayer offered in faith will heal the sick, and the Lord will make you well. And if you have committed any sins, you will be forgiven. (James 5:15)

He heals the brokenhearted and bandages their wounds. (Psalm 147:3)

O LORD, if you heal me, I will be truly healed; if you save me, I will be truly saved. My praises are for you alone! (Jeremiah 17:14)

- **Renewal:**

  This means that anyone who belongs to Christ has become a new person. The old life is gone; a new life has begun! (2 Corinthians 5:17)

  Sin is no longer your master, for you no longer live under the requirements of the law. Instead, you live under the freedom of God's grace. (Romans 6:14)

  And we know that God causes everything to work together for the good of those who love God and are called according to his purpose for them. (Romans 8:28)

  But if we confess our sins to him, he is faithful and just to forgive us our sins and to cleanse us from all wickedness. (1 John 1:9)

- **Salvation:**

  They replied, "Believe in the Lord Jesus and you will be saved, along with everyone in your household." (Acts 16:31)

If you openly declare that Jesus is Lord and believe in your heart that God raised him from the dead, you will be saved. For it is by believing in your heart that you are made right with God, and it is by openly declaring your faith that you are saved. (Romans 10:9–10)

"I tell you the truth, those who listen to my message and believe in God who sent me have eternal life. They will never be condemned for their sins, but they have already passed from death into life. (John 5:24)

"And anyone who believes in God's Son has eternal life. Anyone who doesn't obey the Son will never experience eternal life but remains under God's angry judgment." (John 3:36)

And I am convinced that nothing can ever separate us from God's love. Neither death nor life, neither angels nor demons, neither our fears for today nor our worries about tomorrow—not even the powers of hell can separate us from God's love. No power in the sky above or in the earth below—indeed, nothing in all creation will ever be able to separate us from the love of God that is revealed in Christ Jesus our Lord. (Romans 8:38–39)

(For a downloadable version of the above list of complete Scripture passages, see www.Breakthrough-Book.com.)

# GOD'S POWER IN A PROBLEM

## *The Woman Caught in Adultery*
John 8:1–11

Jesus returned to the Mount of Olives, but early the next morning he was back again at the Temple. A crowd soon gathered, and he sat down and taught them. As he was speaking, the teachers of religious law and the Pharisees brought a woman who had been caught in the act of adultery. They put her in front of the crowd.

"Teacher," they said to Jesus, "this woman was caught in the act of adultery. The law of Moses says to stone her. What do you say?"

They were trying to trap him into saying something they could use against him, but Jesus stooped down and wrote in the dust with his finger. They kept demanding an answer, so he stood up again and said, "All right, but let the one who has never sinned throw the first stone!" Then he stooped down again and wrote in the dust.

When the accusers heard this, they slipped away one by one, beginning with the oldest, until only Jesus was left in the middle of the crowd with the woman. Then Jesus stood up again and said to the woman, "Where are your accusers? Didn't even one of them condemn you?"

"No, Lord," she said.

And Jesus said, "Neither do I. Go and sin no more."

CHAPTER 6

# FINDING PURPOSE IN YOUR PROBLEMS

The apostle Peter knew what it meant to have problems. Peter was interrogated, beaten, thrown into prison and eventually crucified upside down. One thing Peter understood well was that the problems he faced in life served a greater purpose. He wrote:

*Dear friends, don't be surprised*
*at the fiery trials you are going through, as*
*if something strange were happening to you.*
*Instead, be very glad—for these trials make you*
*partners with Christ in his suffering, so that*
*you will have the wonderful joy of seeing his*
*glory when it is revealed to all the world.*
(1 Peter 4:12–13)

Jesus endured a humiliating death on the cross. Though He was completely innocent, blameless of all sin, Jesus suffered at the hands of cruel men. But oh, for what a great purpose! It was through that awful crucifixion that God worked out His gracious will for human history: the conquering of sin and death and the salvation of all who believe in His Son.

As I've underscored throughout these pages, God loves you and wants to give you His power for a breakthrough when you face a problem. If you cooperate with Him and trust His Holy Spirit to guide you, He can turn every problem you face into a possibility for greater intimacy with Him—and an opportunity for greater purpose.

---

God specializes in bringing good out of evil, purpose out of problems, and breakthroughs out of dead ends.

---

Whatever problem you're facing right now, you don't need to lose hope. God specializes in bringing good out of evil, purpose out of problems, and breakthroughs out of dead ends. And while there could be many reasons why God lets us walk through difficulties—after all, His ways are mysterious—there are a few common, possible purposes that would be helpful to keep at the forefront of your mind when everything about your problem seems pointless.

## POSSIBLE PURPOSE: TO TEACH YOU TO TRUST

I (C.A.) have had the blessing of going on several traveling adventures with my family. In my memory, one trip—actually, a particular day on that one trip—is more vivid than any other because of what it taught me about trust. Envision this with me:

It was early afternoon. My dad and I stood face-to-face on a mound of packed, wet mud. We were panting mirror images—hands on hips, foreheads creased in consternation. My best friend, whom I'd taken on the trip with us, was beside a gnarled tree, clutching her hip in a fit of breathy laughter. It was funny, verging on the ridiculous.

The three of us were on a tour of the Costa Rican jungle. Though the rest of the tour group had gone ahead, climbing higher into the jungle canopy, we had stayed behind because Dad thought it improbable that we'd survive climbing the rope ladder that had taken the rest of our companions up into the reaches of paradise. Our tour guide, David, told us to stay put while he led the rest of the group to the next stopping point, assuring us that he'd come back to get us—but he had been gone a long time. We'd tried calling out his name. No answer.

When our voices gave out, Dad and I entered a comical stare-off, a what-do-we-do-now moment of hysteria and an unspoken challenge of who could be more dramatic. (My dad likes to call *me* the most theatrical in the family, but there's little doubt which parent I got that from.) He was the first to crack. Soon, I was trembling trying not to burst with laughter. While our tour guide's seeming abandonment struck us as funny, we were both anxious and ready to leave, and we were playing it up.

"We need to take the horses," Dad said, with a tone strikingly reminiscent of Indiana Jones.

"Yes," I agreed, heart pounding. "We'll take the horses. Let's run!"

Stumbling off the dirt mound, we speedily hiked our way back to the path where we'd tied the horses earlier that morning. My best friend, dumbfounded, eyes glistening with humor, leapt to her feet and followed.

We ran, thinking that once we found the horses, we could ride back to the tour's starting point at the edge of the jungle and wait for David there. We were determined.

But before long, we heard feet padding, breath heaving, hard. David appeared behind us just as we got within reach of the horses' harnesses. He had been chasing us.

He called out to us, "Man, you guys move fast!"

There was a pause among the four of us. Dad seemed impressed at David's effort to locate us. In his lawyerly manner, he cleared his throat and stated our complaint.

"You left us, David."

David shook his head. Slowly, he said, "I was coming right back to help you up. I told you that."

No one spoke. David *had* told us that, but our fear had spoken louder.

We didn't trust David. We didn't trust the jungle. And we certainly didn't trust ourselves, despite our false confidence, to make it to our destination alone. But if we'd stayed where David had told us to, if we'd waited, not only would he have come back for us, but he would've led us to a safer path where we could've climbed for a grand view of God's cloudless sky.

Here's the thing: Sometimes God will allow us to face a problem that overwhelms us so we'll realize our self-sufficiency is just a façade, so we'll come to depend on Him more. Not just depend on Him for our salvation, but for everything—complete dependence in every area of our lives. Learning dependence, in turn, grows our faith. The apostle Paul experienced this:

> *We were crushed and overwhelmed beyond our ability to endure, and we thought we would never live through it. In fact, we expected to die. But as a result, we stopped relying on ourselves and learned to rely only on God, who raises the dead. And he did rescue us from mortal danger, and he will rescue us again. We have placed our confidence in him, and he will continue to rescue us.* (2 Corinthians 1:8–9)

God allowed Paul's problem to overwhelm him. Why? So that Paul would realize he needed God and that he could trust Him. When Paul turned to Him, he experienced God's incredible power—power strong enough to raise the dead.

What problem is crushing you right now? Maybe God is allowing you to go through that hardship so you will finally see your great need for Him, so that you'll surrender and place your trust in Him. As the Old Testament prophet Nahum wrote in Nahum 1:7, "The LORD is good, a strong refuge when trouble comes. He is close to those who trust in him."

## POSSIBLE PURPOSE: TO TEACH YOU TO LEARN FROM OTHERS

The comedian Groucho Marx once quipped, "Learn from the mistakes of others. You can never live long enough to make them all yourself." Most of us would agree if pressed that we'd rather learn to avoid a pit by watching someone else fall into it than fall into the pit ourselves. The problem is that sometimes we're too stubborn to humble ourselves enough to learn from the people around us. We don't like to admit that we need help or that we're wrong. But Scripture repeatedly tells us that if we're obstinate and unwilling to learn from others, we're headed for trouble.

Instead, when we let others help us, particularly those in God's family, they can raise us to a new level. Proverbs 27:17 says, "As iron sharpens iron, so a friend sharpens a friend." The key is to surround yourself with godly people—and the best way to do that is by being involved in a strong, Bible-based church. When you're involved in a good church, the people around you can help you through your problems, if you'll let them. It's likely some of them have already gone through what you're dealing with, or something similar, and they've come out on the other side. If you ask for their help instead of isolating yourself, they can help you avoid the same pit that they fell into.

I'm always amazed that, for almost every problem I face, there is someone in our church who has faced the same problem and found a breakthrough. We often miss out on these human resources that God has placed around us because we stand on the sidelines, afraid to be vulnerable. But when we engage in our church by becoming a member, serving with others, joining a small group Bible study, or simply making it a point to meet other people, God can miraculously put the people we need right in front of us.

---

I'm always amazed that, for almost every problem I face, there is someone in our church who has faced the same problem and found a breakthrough.

---

One of the side effects of my chemotherapy has been neuropathy in my feet and fingertips. *Neuropathy* means that you don't have full nerve response (feeling) in your feet and hands. For me, my feet feel like they are constantly asleep, and I have to be careful walking because I can easily trip on uneven pavement or on cords on a crowded stage. I have never shared this side effect with my whole church when teaching or during a large gathering since I don't want every story I tell to be about my cancer. After all, I am not defined by cancer or even my status as a cancer survivor, even though it's a critical part of my life story.

Not too long ago, at a small seminar our church hosted for some of our top servers and volunteers, I sat in the audience taking notes like everyone else. During a break, someone serendipitously said something about my new shoes. (I use the word *serendipitously* not only for fancy-word bonus points but also to set up that this little conversation was more of a God thing than an offhanded compliment.) I mentioned briefly that I was testing them out because they are designed for folks with neuropathy. One of our regular servers overheard and said, "I have neuropathy in my feet too." This guy is on our parking lot and greeting team and probably burns more calories on a Sunday than anyone else because he's always on the move. I was floored. He then pulled over another young lady and told me she had neuropathy too. They'd just been talking about it a few weeks before. Both began sharing their best practices for dealing with the issue. They talked about how to train yourself to watch your steps so you can avoid tripping. They also told me how to manage the medications, gave me some ideas for what to wear to minimize discomfort, and shared tips on how to handle major flare-ups that sometimes occur.

I've seen similar scenarios play out with other people facing various problems in our church. For example, a friend who was facing a difficult parenting challenge recently discovered there was someone else in our church who had walked through that same challenge and was able to share insight and wisdom on how to handle it. Reread that previous sentence and change *parenting challenge* to *legal challenge* or *business challenge*, or even one time it was a *NYC marathon challenge*. No matter what you're facing, there is likely someone in your church family who has been there.

---

He may allow a problem to persist in your life to remind you that you need godly people around you and to help you recognize that you must be open to learning from others.

---

God wants to work through the body of Christ to provide you with the support and wisdom that can catalyze the breakthrough you're praying for. Sometimes that's God's purpose behind the problem you're dealing with. He may allow a problem to persist in your life to remind you that you need godly people around you and to help you recognize that you must be open to learning from others.

(Mind you, I still don't burn as many calories running around on a Sunday as my neuropathy compatriot, but his advice has been invaluable.)

## POSSIBLE PURPOSE: TO TEACH YOU TO ADJUST YOUR PRIORITIES

God doesn't want second place in your life. He wants first place; He deserves first place. But because we're finite, fickle creatures, it's easy for our priorities to get out of alignment. Often, we end up putting work, money, or even another person ahead of God. None of those things are bad in and of themselves, but when we place any one of them ahead of God, they become a problem. They become what the Bible calls an idol. If you are making something other than God an idol, He may remove that thing from your life. (For in-depth reading on viewing and handling money God's way, see my book *The Generosity Secret: How to Get Out of Debt and Find Financial Freedom*. Learn more at www.Breakthrough-Book.com.)

We often end up dealing with problems longer than we need to because we refuse to put God first and take His commandments seriously. Jesus addressed this in His Sermon on the Mount, commanding His followers to "seek the Kingdom of God above all else, and live righteously, and he will give you everything you need" (Matthew 6:33). Seeking God's Kingdom above all else can help us avoid the heartbreak we too often encounter when our priorities become misaligned.

The 19th-century British evangelist George Müller knew what it was to put God first and trust His provision. George was passionate about taking care of orphaned children. One night, he and the children in the orphanage he had started discovered that their food pantry was empty. Everything had been eaten. But even in the face of starvation, George clasped his hands together and prayed, thanking God—remember what we talked about in chapter 2 about starting prayer with gratitude—for all that He would supply them.

At that moment, a knock sounded at the door. A baker had woken his apprentices in the night to bake bread for George and the children after having a dream. Then another man came to them, saying the axle of his wagon had broken, and he needed to dispense with his milk before it spoiled.

I'm sure George was familiar with Jesus' words as recorded by Matthew. They certainly came alive for him that night. The command bears repeating:

"Seek the Kingdom of God **above all else**, and live righteously, and **he will give you everything you need**" (Matthew 6:33, emphasis added).

## POSSIBLE PURPOSE: TO MAKE YOU MORE LIKE JESUS

Learning to trust God, learning from others in God's family, adjusting our priorities to put God first—all these things grow us more and more into Jesus' likeness every day. These are key practices that God will use to provide the breakthrough for the problems we're facing as we lean into Him and the guidance of His Holy Spirit.

Jesus is the perfect image of His Father, and He is the one we should strive to model our hearts, minds and lives after. Though we will never be Jesus, with God's help, we can grow more and more in godliness every day. This is exactly what Paul was talking about in his letter to the Christians in Ephesus:

> *Since you have heard about Jesus and have learned the truth that comes from him, throw off your old sinful nature and your former way of life, which is corrupted by lust and deception. Instead, let the Spirit renew your thoughts and attitudes. Put on your new nature, created to be like God—truly righteous and holy.* (Ephesians 4:21–24)

God uses all kinds of things in your life to move you in that direction. He's using your church to help you become more like Jesus as well as your quiet time with Him, your Bible study and your godly friends and mentors. And yes, He's even using your problems to make you more like His Son. As the great British preacher Charles Spurgeon once said of suffering:

*Our joy is like the wave as it dashes on the shore—it throws us on the earth. But our sorrows are like that receding wave which sucks us back again into the great depth of godhead. We should have been stranded and left high and dry on the shore if it had not been for that receding wave, that ebbing of our prosperity, which carried us back to our Father and our God again.*[7]

Stated another way, our suffering drives us back to dependence on God, and that is something to rejoice over, especially knowing that God uses everything we're walking through to make us more like Jesus.

---

7 Charles Spurgeon, "The Sweet Uses of Adversity," *New Park Street Pulpit*, vol. 5, November 13, 1859, The Spurgeon Center, https://www.spurgeon.org /resource-library/sermons/the-sweet-uses-of-adversity/#flipbook/.

Shining in the likeness of the Son is the best breakthrough we could ever experience!

*We can rejoice, too, when we run into problems and trials for we know that they help us develop endurance. And endurance develops strength of character, and character strengthens our confident hope of salvation.* (Romans 5:3)

---

Shining in the likeness of the Son is the best breakthrough we could ever experience!

---

(For more resources to help you discover God's purpose for your life, see www.Breakthrough-Book.com.)

# GOD'S POWER IN A PROBLEM

*The Resurrection*
Matthew 28:1–10

Early on Sunday morning, as the new day was dawning, Mary Magdalene and the other Mary went out to visit the tomb.

Suddenly there was a great earthquake! For an angel of the Lord came down from heaven, rolled aside the stone, and sat on it. His face shone like lightning, and his clothing was as white as snow. The guards shook with fear when they saw him, and they fell into a dead faint.

Then the angel spoke to the women. "Don't be afraid!" he said. "I know you are looking for Jesus, who was crucified. He isn't here! He is risen from the dead, just as he said would happen. Come, see where his body was lying. And now, go quickly and tell his disciples that he has risen from the dead, and he is going ahead

133

of you to Galilee. You will see him there. Remember what I have told you."

The women ran quickly from the tomb. They were very frightened but also filled with great joy, and they rushed to give the disciples the angel's message. And as they went, Jesus met them and greeted them. And they ran to him, grasped his feet, and worshiped him. Then Jesus said to them, "Don't be afraid! Go tell my brothers to leave for Galilee, and they will see me there."

## CHAPTER 7

# HOW TO PERSEVERE

What are the three biggest problems you're dealing with right now? I encourage you to write them down. There's power when pen hits paper. Be honest with yourself and write out the three things you worry about most.

What is keeping you up at night?

What do you find yourself complaining about constantly?

What are you worried about this very minute?

What do you keep replaying in your mind, no matter what else is going on around you?

Maybe it's an illness. Maybe it's a financial problem. Maybe you're wrestling with depression that won't break or an addiction that won't let you go. Maybe a loved one is struggling and you're feeling the effects. Maybe it's a personal problem you've never told anyone about, something you've handled but it keeps popping back up. Some problems seem to linger and resurface like that. No matter what you do or how earnestly you pray, they seemingly won't go away. (For more on finding strength to stand in the face of life's problems, see my book *Unshakable: Standing Strong When Things Go Wrong*. To learn how to secure your own copy or how to utilize the book with your small group, see www.Breakthrough-Book.com.)

Lately, I (C.A.) have felt the weight of problems that won't seem to go away. The problems in my life and in the lives of those I love keep growing, shifting, settling and then growing again, never fully subsiding. But in what felt like a moment of direct encouragement from God, I happened to come across the poem "No Coward Soul Is Mine," written by the British author Emily Brontë in 1846:

> *No coward soul is mine*
> *No trembler in the world's storm-troubled sphere*
> *I see Heaven's glories shine*
> *And Faith shines equal arming me from Fear*
>
> *O God within my breast*
> *Almighty ever-present Deity*
> *Life, that in me hast rest,*
> *As I Undying Life, have power in Thee*
>
> *Vain are the thousand creeds*
> *That move men's hearts, unutterably vain,*

*Worthless as withered weeds*
*Or idlest froth amid the boundless main*

*To waken doubt in one*
*Holding so fast by thy infinity,*
*So surely anchored on*
*The steadfast rock of Immortality.*

*With wide-embracing love*
*Thy spirit animates eternal years*
*Pervades and broods above,*
*Changes, sustains, dissolves, creates and rears*

*Though earth and moon were gone*
*And suns and universes ceased to be*
*And Thou wert left alone*
*Every Existence would exist in thee*

*There is not room for Death*
*Nor atom that his might could render void*
*Since thou art Being and Breath*
*And what thou art may never be destroyed.*[8]

What Emily understood with a keen, eternal per-spective is that God is faithful beyond our compre-hension. We can persevere in this life because He is

8    Emily Brontë, "No Coward Soul Is Mine," *Poems by Currer, Ellis and Acton Bell*
     (London: Aylott and Jones, 1846).

the author and finisher of our faith (Hebrews 12:2). He sustains us, and He will see us through to the very end. The apostle James wrote about this kind of godly perseverance: "When troubles of any kind come your way, consider it an opportunity for great joy. For you know that when your faith is tested, your endurance has a chance to grow" (James 1:2–3).

Problems produce great endurance in us. They shape us for God's glory. Best of all, when we believe in Jesus, God gives us the power of the Holy Spirit to strengthen and guide us through all of life's difficulties. We could be going through the worst moments imaginable, overcome by the burden of our troubles, but amid it all, we can know that God is with us. He is more than able and willing to help us walk through anything. And best of all, nothing can separate us from His love. As the apostle Paul wrote:

*Can anything ever separate us from*
*Christ's love? Does it mean he no longer*
*loves us if we have trouble or calamity, or*
*are persecuted, or hungry, or destitute, or*
*in danger, or threatened with death?...*
*No, despite all these things, overwhelming*
*victory is ours through Christ, who loved us.*
(Romans 8:35, 37)

With that incredible reality in mind, here are three final steps we can take to help us persevere during difficult times as we trust God for our breakthrough:

- Remember God's faithfulness.

- Refocus on spiritual growth.

- Renew your commitment to Jesus.

Let's look at each one in more detail.

---

Problems produce great endurance in us.
They shape us for God's glory.

---

## REMEMBER GOD'S FAITHFULNESS

To persevere through whatever problem you're facing right now, it's so helpful to remember God's faithfulness to you in the past. Think back to all the times God has already moved mountains for you.

It's important to be intentional about remembering God's faithfulness because when our vision becomes blurred by a new problem, we tend to have a short memory span. We become consumed with what's in front of us and forget the miracles we've seen in our past. We forget what God can do and what He's already done.

---

Even though our struggles can sometimes seem like dismissiveness on God's part, we must trust in His character—His righteous character that is proven again and again in Scripture and in our own experience.

---

That's what happened to the Israelites in the Old Testament. They had been in slavery for 400 years in Egypt. God rescued them from Egypt, then led them to the promised land. He performed incredible miracles along the way. As the Egyptians pursued the Israelites, God parted the Red Sea so they could walk through it. He took them to the desert, provided water where there was none, and rained food from the sky. He took them to the Jordan River, in view of the promised land.

All the blessing He wanted to give them was on the other side of that river. But His people looked across the river, and all they saw was a problem: an enemy. The enemy was formidable, there were many of them, and they had weapons and walled cities to defend the land. Despite the fact God had just parted a sea for them to walk across, killing other enemies in the process, they wanted to give up. They were ready to turn around, go back to Egypt, and be slaves again. But Moses told them, "But don't be afraid of them! Just remember what the LORD your God did to Pharaoh and to all the land of Egypt" (Deuteronomy 7:18).

He told them to *remember*—remember who God is and what He's already done. We need to do this too. We need to look back on our own lives and remember God's faithfulness, and we also need to go to His Word to remember His faithfulness to His people throughout history. A note of caution: while God is faithful, that doesn't mean He always removes a problem in the way the people involved think He should. Remember, His ways are higher than ours, and the circumstances and obstacles in our lives serve purposes we may never fully understand. Jeremiah 29:11 says, " 'For I know the plans I have for you,' says the LORD. 'They are plans for good and not for disaster, to give you a future and a hope.' "

Even though our struggles can sometimes seem like dismissiveness on God's part, we must trust in His character—His righteous character that is proven again and again in Scripture and in our own experience. We will continue to live in a world broken by sin, but God is good, all the time.

## REFOCUS ON SPIRITUAL GROWTH

I can't tell you how many times someone has come up to me and said something like "You know, I haven't been to church in a while because I'm having some problems with my girlfriend, so I've just been focusing on that instead of coming to church." Or "Work has been so overwhelming, so I'm skipping Bible study this semester." Or "You know, I'm feeling depressed. I just can't get out of it. I've taken a break from serving so I can focus on myself."

In other words, what we do when we're suffering is often the exact opposite of what we need to be doing to persevere and grow in godliness. We remove the things that are going to grow us and give us strength. But because He's good, God has given us a promise: "Come close to God, and God will come close to you" (James 4:8). If you allow Him, God will grow you spiritually through your problem. He will strengthen you. As I've mentioned, He will use it to make you more like His Son, Jesus.

This growing into Jesus' likeness doesn't happen automatically. Thankfully, believers have the Holy Spirit in them enabling their growth in God. But we must also participate in it. We should stay engaged with spiritual habits—meet with God, confess our sin, and place the whole of our lives before Him to change and mold and shape however He wants. And we don't do this alone. God's family, the church, is with us in this godly persevering too.

One of the biggest mistakes we could make when a problem hits us is give up on the very things we need to get through the pain. If a problem is causing us to lose focus on our spiritual growth, then we need to stop and seek God, as 1 Chronicles 16:11 directs us: "Search for the LORD and for his strength; continually seek him." We need to stop, pray, open His Word, and allow Him to guide us to growth through the trials we face.

## RENEW YOUR COMMITMENT TO JESUS

Despite what many people may think, following Jesus isn't just about making a one-time commitment. Yes, there is that first moment when you ask Jesus to come into your life, forgive you of your sins and save you. That is a standing commitment that assures your sins are forgiven, that you will now have the Holy Spirit within you and that you will see God in heaven.

But the commitment to follow Jesus, to daily make Him the leader and Lord of your life even through the most difficult parts of your life, that's a commitment you have to renew sometimes hourly, sometimes every minute. Daunting as that may seem, recall Jesus' promise in Matthew 11:28: "Come to me all of you who are weary and carry heavy burdens, and I will give you rest." He wants us to come to Him over and over, to lay down our problems at His feet and recommit to His lordship in our lives.

---

But the commitment to follow
Jesus, to daily make Him the leader and
Lord of your life even through the most difficult
parts of your life, that's a commitment
you have to renew sometimes hourly,
sometimes every minute.

---

If you're carrying a heavy burden, give it to Jesus, and He will carry it for you. Recommit yourself to Him. Commit everything you are and everything you have to Him. Then, tomorrow, when heaviness descends on your heart again, give everything over to Him again. Then do it again. And *again*. Sometimes I have to give Jesus the same problem 20 to 25 times in a single day. But, trust me, there is no other Savior than Jesus Christ, and life from His upside-down perspective offers a view beyond the scope of your wildest imagination.

God is the best person to bring any and all of our burdens to because He never gets tired. We can rest in His status as Sovereign, ruler of all, trusting that He's going to bring about the breakthrough He desires for us in His time as we trust and cooperate with His ways.

# TRUST GOD FOR YOUR BREAKTHROUGH

My prayer is that this book has reminded you of the ultimate hope that allows you to triumph over life's problems: the hope our Lord Jesus Christ won for us at the cross and through His resurrection. Now that you've made it to the end, my final challenge to you is this: Continue to trust God for your breakthrough.

Keeping in mind all we've discussed, take another look at our working definition of a breakthrough:

**A *breakthrough* is when God grows you deeper in your relationship with Jesus, through the power of the Holy Spirit, by providing a biblical solution to the problem you're facing.**

Together in these pages, we have explored six biblical mindsets and tools that, when applied through the leading of the Holy Spirit, will allow you to access God's solution for your problem—your breakthrough—while drawing you closer to Jesus in the process. Here they are again:

1. Prayer
2. Perspective
3. Peace
4. Promises
5. Purpose
6. Perseverance

These six tools are the key elements that will enable you to discover God's breakthrough no matter what kind of problem you're facing. Sometimes, you'll need to be mindful in all six areas before your breakthrough comes. Other times, God will show you your breakthrough as you take just one or two of these to heart.

For some, it has taken prayer, a transformed perspective and a deep-rooted reliance on the promises God lays out in Scripture before they have received a breakthrough for their problem. Mind you, their breakthrough didn't come simply because they checked boxes in these areas—God is not Santa Claus, a jolly old man who grants our requests when we behave well. Their breakthrough came when it did because they learned whatever it was God wanted to teach them through that season of hardship.

For others, it has taken prayer, a transformed perspective, a whole new understanding of purpose and a relentless perseverance through pain before their prayers were answered. Again, not because they had some correct combination or ticked these things from a to-do list. No, they leaned into these areas with open hearts, and God chose to bless them and their walk in faith.

---

When you are walking with Jesus and living in light of these six principles and mindsets, you will begin to transform from the inside out.

---

I think the best breakthroughs occur when all these spiritual elements come together in a believer's heart, mind and soul in a supernatural way—that in and of itself is a breakthrough, of sorts. When you are walking with Jesus and living in light of these six principles and mindsets, you will begin to transform from the inside out. You will know beyond a shadow of a doubt that God is with you, even if you aren't seeing an external break in your circumstances.

In some situations, God brings a breakthrough immediately. In others, it can take a while. We all want to be able to seek God, gain His perspective, ask for His power and, *boom!*...have a breakthrough. And I've seen this happen many times. More often, however, breakthroughs take a few weeks, a few months, or even a few years. I wanted my cancer to be cured immediately, but instead it was a three-year process entailing multiple surgeries. I've known many Christians who pray for a loved one to trust in Jesus as their Savior, invite them to church repeatedly and share their faith clearly for years (long after I might have given up) until that person does eventually repent and believe. I've seen people beg God *to do it now*—whatever *it* is—yet God seems silent and slow. I would argue that He was working on them *and* the problem in ways they couldn't immediately know or discern.

As one of my mentors taught me, there's no such thing as instant maturity in this life. If you are working on a serious relationship problem, for example, God could bring a breakthrough immediately, but He may move slowly because you need to mature, or because trust can only be restored over time. God may choose to delay the breakthrough, not because His power is limited or because He doesn't desire ultimate healing for all brokenness, but because His view of our problems is more profound and His solution more comprehensive; He needs to work on us first so that His breakthrough will be sustained when He gives it.

Then there are the breakthroughs that we never see in this life. As stated over and over in previous chapters, God's ways are not our ways. This was the apostle Paul's experience. Paul, a spiritual giant, great leader of the early church and author of much of the New Testament, never got the breakthrough he so desperately prayed for throughout his life. Paul had an unspecified problem that he called a *thorn in the flesh*. We know through Scripture that he begged God to take it away. The best scholarship tells us that God never removed the problem. Paul didn't get his breakthrough on this side of eternity, which makes him the perfect person to offer us hope when we find ourselves in a situation that seems like it is never going to change:

> *So to keep me from becoming proud, I was given a thorn in my flesh.... Three different times I begged the Lord to take it away. Each time he said,* **"My grace is all you need. My power works best in weakness."** *So now I am glad to boast about my weaknesses, so that the power of Christ can work through me.*

*That's why I take pleasure in my weaknesses,
and in the insults, hardships, persecutions, and
troubles that I suffer for Christ. For when I
am weak, then I am strong.* (2 Corinthians
12:7–10, emphasis added)

The truth in Paul's words is profound. The breakthrough he was hoping for didn't come, but he matured to the place of being able to boast in his weaknesses because they demonstrated the power of Christ through him. Again, that type of growth is truly a breakthrough in its own right.

---

No matter what situation you're facing
right now, God is more than capable of
lightening the burden. Give it to Him.

---

If you're a follower of Jesus, but you've let your problems dim the light of God's love toward you, I invite you to renew your commitment to Him. No matter what situation you're facing right now, God is more than capable of lightening the burden. Give it to Him. Cooperate with what He wants to do in your life by applying what you've learned in these pages and asking the Holy Spirit to guide you into the growth

God has for you. He loves you beyond measure. He is working everything together for your good. Run back to Him and ask Him for your breakthrough.

If you've never accepted Jesus into your life and trusted Him as your Lord and Savior, there is no better time than right now. When you do, you will be miraculously reconciled to the God who so lovingly created you. You'll be given the Holy Spirit; embark on an incredible, transformative relationship with God here on earth; and be assured of an eternity with Him in heaven. Wherever you are, pray this prayer of surrender with me now:

> *Father, I recognize I'm broken and there is nothing I can do to fix myself or my problems. I see now who You are and how much I need You. I believe that You sent Your Son, Jesus Christ, to live a sinless life on earth, die a criminal's death on the cross and rise again three days later, conquering sin and death. I invite Jesus into my heart now, and though I know I've done nothing to deserve it, I ask You to cleanse me of my sin, gift me Your Holy Spirit and assure me of my eternity in heaven. I don't want to be separate from You anymore in this life or in the next. I surrender to You. I pray this in Jesus' name. Amen.*

If you just prayed that prayer from your heart, you are now a permanent part of God's beloved family. Welcome! I encourage you to find a nearby Bible-based church and introduce yourself to the pastor so you can be discipled in loving community. I would also encourage you to share this decision with your pastor or a Christian friend. (For more resources to help you grow in Christ, see www.Breakthrough-Book.com.)

In Revelation, the final book of the Bible, the apostle John described heaven:

> *Look, God's home is now among his people!*
> *He will live with them, and they will be his*
> *people. God himself will be with them. He will*
> *wipe every tear from their eyes and there will*
> *be no more death or sorrow or crying or pain.*
> *All these things are gone forever.* (21:3–4)

In heaven, believers will feel God's presence continually; we will be with Him all the time. No more separation, no more death, no more sorrow, no more crying, no more pain. Just think of it! Every problem we've had to face in this life—gone. In its place, God Himself. That is what awaits all those who believe in Jesus Christ. That is the ultimate breakthrough.

# A FINAL NOTE
# FROM NELSON

I hope this book will be the beginning of an ongoing conversation. Please visit www.Breakthrough-Book.com to connect with me or my co-authors, access many free resources and share your breakthrough story.

Also, remember that problems will continue to come regardless of physical age or spiritual maturity. Keep this book handy and return to these principles and the following appendix material as needed.

Finally, if these principles have helped you, consider sharing a copy with a friend. Or go deeper and use this book as a small group study in your church. Talk with your pastor and then visit www.Breakthrough-Book.com for discount information when you secure multiple copies of this book.

# 30-DAY PATH TO BREAKTHROUGH WORKSHEET

**Remember: A *breakthrough* is when God grows you deeper in your relationship with Jesus, through the power of the Holy Spirit, by providing a biblical solution to the problem you're facing.**

Let's take the breakthrough principles that you just discovered and apply them over the next 30 days to a specific situation in your life.

- Take a moment and select an area of your life where you need a breakthrough (e.g., relational, financial, spiritual, physical, etc.).

———————————————————————————————

(my breakthrough area,
described in two or three words)

• Now, write out the specific problem you identified above in as much detail and with as much clarity as possible. The more specific you can define the problem, the more you can experience God's breakthrough power in this problem.

———————————————————————————————
———————————————————————————————
———————————————————————————————
———————————————————————————————
———————————————————————————————
———————————————————————————————
———————————————————————————————
———————————————————————————————
———————————————————————————————
———————————————————————————————
———————————————————————————————
———————————————————————————————
———————————————————————————————
———————————————————————————————
———————————————————————————————

- Take a full 10 minutes and go to God in prayer, talking with Him about the problem you just outlined. Begin with thanksgiving, then turn to presenting your problem to God, and now boldly ask Him for a breakthrough in this area over the next 30 days. Then conclude with submitting to God's will (not yours), in Jesus' name!

- Congratulations, you are on the way toward the breakthrough solution that God has for your problem! Consider this the end of Day 1.

- For Days 2–30, set aside 10–15 minutes each day, ideally when you first arise, but pick a time when you are alert and won't be interrupted.

- Begin each time with a general breakthrough prayer and then work through just one of the six areas of breakthrough, talking and listening to God as you go.

- Continue to sequentially work through all six areas, repeating as many times as possible until you receive your breakthrough or the 30-day period ends.

  - **Area 1–Prayer:** Open your prayer time with thanksgiving and review your problem with God, while both talking and listening to

God. Remember that prayer is an important part of the remaining five areas, so return to chapter 2 as needed to grow in your understanding of prayer.

○ **Area 2–Perspective:** Ask God to give you the proper perspective on your problem. (Review chapter 3 as needed.)

○ **Area 3–Peace:** Ask God to give you His supernatural peace of heart, mind and soul as you seek your breakthrough. (Review chapter 4 as needed.)

○ **Area 4–Promises:** Remind God of His promises to you, and claim those promises as you pray for breakthrough. (Review chapter 5 as needed, and see also the Scriptures in appendices B and C.)

○ **Area 5–Purpose:** Ask God to show you His purposes in your problem. How does God want to grow you as He guides you toward a breakthrough? (Review chapter 6 as needed.)

○ **Area 6–Perseverance:** Ask God to give you the strength to continue to persevere and stand strong as you see God's solution for your problem and experience your breakthrough. (Review chapter 7 as needed.)

- Once you experience your breakthrough, take time to thank God and celebrate how your breakthrough has brought you closer to God. You might share your breakthrough with another Christian, your Bible study group, or your pastor.

- Be encouraged by these words from the apostle Paul as he was seeking a breakthrough:

> *So to keep me from becoming proud, I was given a thorn in my flesh.... Three different times I begged the Lord to take it away. Each time he said, **"My grace is all you need. My power works best in weakness."** So now I am glad to boast about my weaknesses, so that the power of Christ can work through me. That's why I take pleasure in my weaknesses, and in the insults, hardships, persecutions, and troubles that I suffer for Christ. For when I am weak, then I am strong.*
> (2 Corinthians 12:7–10 emphasis added)

- Return to this worksheet for guidance when you need a future breakthrough.

(For a free downloadable version of this worksheet, visit www.Breakthrough-Book.com.)

# MEMORY VERSE SUGGESTIONS FOR EACH CHAPTER

Memorizing Scripture is one of the greatest ways to grow in your relationship with God, to give you the spiritual strength for a breakthrough when you face a problem, and to keep you on the right path to avoid future problems. Here are some recommended Scriptures to memorize from each chapter.

## Introduction

*So be strong and courageous! Do not be afraid and do not panic before them. For the LORD your God will personally go ahead of you. He will neither fail you, nor abandon you.* (Deuteronomy 31:6)

## Chapter 1: What Not to Do When You Have a Problem

*We are pressed on every side by troubles, but we are not crushed. We are perplexed, but not driven to despair. We are hunted down, but never abandoned by God. We get knocked down, but we are not destroyed. Through suffering, our bodies continue to share in the death of Jesus so that the life of Jesus may also be seen in our bodies.* (2 Corinthians 4:8–10)

## Chapter 2: Pray, Then Pray Again

*Don't worry about anything; instead, pray about everything. Tell God what you need, and thank him for all he has done. Then you will experience God's peace, which exceeds anything we can understand. His peace will guard your hearts and minds as you live in Christ Jesus.* (Philippians 4:6–7)

## Chapter 3: Keeping Your Problems in Perspective

*Dear brothers and sisters, when troubles of any kind come your way, consider it an opportunity for great joy. For you know that when your faith is tested, your endurance has a chance to grow. So let it grow, for when your endurance is fully developed, you will be perfect and complete, needing nothing.* (James 1:2–4)

## Chapter 4: Knowing God's Peace

*I [Jesus] am leaving you with a gift—peace of mind and heart. And the peace I give is a gift the world cannot give. So don't be troubled or afraid.* (John 14:27)

## Chapter 5: God, the Promise Keeper

*Anyone who listens to my teaching and follows it is wise, like a person who builds a house on solid rock. Though the rain comes in torrents and the floodwaters rise and the winds beat against that house, it won't collapse because it is built on bedrock. But anyone who hears my teaching and doesn't obey it is foolish, like a person who builds a house on sand. When the rains and floods come and the winds beat against that house, it will collapse with a mighty crash.* (Matthew 7:24–27)

## Chapter 6: Finding Purpose in Your Problems

*We can rejoice, too, when we run into problems and trials for we know that they help us develop endurance. And endurance develops strength of character, and character strengthens our confident hope of salvation.* (Romans 5:3–4)

## Chapter 7: How to Persevere

*Come close to God, and God will come close to you.* (James 4:8)

## Conclusion: Trusting God for Your Breakthrough

*Look, God's home is now among his people! He will live with them, and they will be his people. God himself will be with them. He will wipe every tear from their eyes, and there will be no more death or sorrow or crying or pain. All these things are gone forever.* (Revelation 21:3–4)

# SCRIPTURES TO STUDY FOR BREAKTHROUGH

A s you seek your breakthrough, the breakthrough principles from this book will help, but your most powerful tool for a breakthrough is the words of Scripture. Take each of the Scriptures below and, using your favorite physical Bible, online Bible, or Bible app, locate each one. Read. Reflect. Highlight. Repeat.

- **Guidance:** Psalm 48:14; Psalm 37:4; Isaiah 41:13; Proverbs 3:6; Psalm 32:8

- **Wisdom:** Proverbs 2:6–7; James 1:5

- **Peace:** John 14:27; Romans 5:1; Philippians 4:6–7

- **Strength:** Isaiah 40:29–31; Isaiah 41:10; Philippians 4:13

- **Provision:** Matthew 6:33; Matthew 7:11; Luke 12:22–24; Philippians 4:19

- **Healing:** James 5:15; Psalm 147:3; Jeremiah 17:14

- **Renewal:** 2 Corinthians 5:17; Romans 6:14; Romans 8:28; 1 John 1:9

- **Salvation:** Acts 16:31; Romans 10:9–10; John 5:24; John 3:36; Romans 8:38–39

# SCRIPTURE GUIDE WHERE TO FIND HELP WHEN YOU ARE...

**Afraid:**
Psalm 27:1, 5; 34:4; 56:1–13; 91:1–16; Isaiah 35:4; 41:10; John 14–27; Hebrews 13:6; 1 John 4:18

**Angry:**
Psalm 37:8; Proverbs 14:29; 15:1; Matthew 5:22–24; Romans 12:10–21; Ephesians 4:26, 31–32; James 1:19–20

**Anxious/Worried:**
Psalm 37:5; 46:1–11; 55:22; Proverbs 3:5–6; Matthew 6:25–34; Philippians 4:6–7; 1 Peter 5:7

**Bitter/Resentful:**
Matthew 6:14–15; Romans 12:14–15; 1 Peter 2:23

**Depressed:**
Psalm 27:13–14; 34:1–22; 42:1–11; Isaiah 41:10;
Matthew 11:28–30; Romans 8:28; Philippians 4:13

**Discouraged/Disappointed:**
Matthew 11:28–30; Romans 8:28; 2 Corinthians
4:8–9, 16–18; Galatians 6:9; Phillipians 1:6; 4:6–7,
19; 1 Thessalonians 3:3; Hebrews 10:35–36; 1
Peter 1:6–9

**Distraught/Upset:**
Psalm 31:24; 61:1–2; 103:13–14; Luke 18:1–8;
Hebrews 12:3; 13:5; 1 Peter 5:7

**Doubting:**
John 6:37; 10:27–29; Philippians 1:6;
2 Timothy 1:12; Hebrews 11:6; 12:2; 1 John 5:13

**Far from God:**
Psalm 139:1–18; Proverbs 28:13; Isaiah 55:7;
Lamentations 3:22–23; Luke 15:11–24;
Revelation 2:4–5

## Jealous/Envious:

Exodus 20:17; Proverbs 14:30; 27:4;
1 Corinthians 3:3; Galatians 5:19–21, 26;
Hebrews 13:5; James 3:16; 5:9

## Lonely:

Psalm 25:16–18; Isaiah 46:4; 55:12; John 14:15–21;
Acts 2:25–26; Hebrews 13:5–6

## Mourning:

Psalm 23; Isaiah 25:8; John 11:25; 14:1–3;
1 Corinthians 15:55; 2 Corinthians 5:1;
Philippians 1:21; 1 Thessalonians 4:13–18;
1 Peter 1:3–4

## Sad:

Psalm 91:14–15; 119:50; Isaiah 43:2; 61:1–3;
2 Corinthians 1:3–4; 2 Thessalonians 2:16–17;
Hebrews 4:15–16

## Sick:

Exodus 15:26; 23:25; Psalm 30:2; 41:3; 91:3–10;
103:3–5; 107:20; Jeremiah 30:17; 33:6;
Matthew 9:35; James 5:14–15; 3 John 2

**Tempted:**
Psalm 119:9–11; Matthew 4:1–4,11;
1 Corinthians 10:12–13; James 1:2–3, 12–15; 4:7

**Troubled by Wrong Thoughts:**
Joshua 1:8; Psalm 1:1–6; 4:4; 19:7–14; Isaiah 26:3;
Philippians 4:8; Colossians 3:2

# *UNSHAKABLE: STANDING STRONG WHEN THINGS GO WRONG*

## BY NELSON SEARCY

This book is a companion to an earlier book we wrote entitled *Unshakable: Standing Strong When Things Go Wrong*. While the entire book can be helpful, I think chapter 1 is especially relevant, so it's included here. You can find info on the full book, including discounted copies for small group use, at www. Breakthrough-Book.com.

## CHAPTER 1

# The First Principle of Unshakable Faith

*A man of courage is also full of faith.*

—Marcus Tullius Cicero

*Anyone who listens to my teaching and follows it is wise, like a person who builds a house on solid rock... But anyone who hears my teaching and doesn't obey it is foolish, like a person who builds a house on sand.*

—Jesus (Matthew 7:24,26)

Not long ago, my wife Kelley, my son Alexander, and I were staying at a friend's house. Late one night, after Kelley and Alexander had gone to bed, I decided to make use of my friend's office area to get some work done. As I was settling into the desk chair, I noticed a snake on the ground beside my foot. I froze. Then, doing my best not to disturb it, I slid out of the chair and retreated to the other side of the office. My heart was pounding. There are few things I despise more than snakes.

After some deep breaths to clear my head, I slipped out of the room and rummaged around in a couple of closets until I found a broom. The office had glass doors that opened to the yard (probably how the snake got in), so my plan was to stun the sucker with the handle of the broom, get those glass doors open and sweep it outside... all without getting bitten. I tip-toed back into the office. Sure enough, the snake was right where I had left him. I put my plan into action: Stun. Open. Sweep. It worked! Mission accomplished. The bad news was that I was too rattled to get any work done. When I finally calmed down, I headed to bed.

The next morning, I couldn't wait to tell Kelley how I had saved us from venom comas and certain death. As I poured her a cup of coffee, I said, "You're never going to believe this. There was a snake in the office last night and..."

"Was it a black snake?" she asked.

"Yeah, it was black... I sat down right beside it, but it didn't move. So I eased out of the chair and snuck out of the office and found a broom..."

"Was it about this long?" She held her hands 16 inches or so apart.

"Yes…" I answered, wondering where these questions were coming from. "Anyway, I decided to stun it and then…"

Before I could finish my story, Kelley burst into laughter. I was a little offended by her response to my heroics.

"Why are you laughing," I asked.

"I bought Alex that snake at the toy store yesterday!"

I have to admit, I was embarrassed. Here I was thinking of myself as a snake wrangler on par with Indiana Jones, only to find that my nemesis had been a piece of plastic and rubber. But the whole scenario got me thinking…

Lots of times, we let things shake us that really don't have to. Situations that seem overwhelming at first are often only child's play. We should be able to stay calm enough to step back and see things from the right perspective but, by nature, we default to anxiety—even though God tells us not to be anxious about anything:

> *Don't worry about anything; instead, pray about everything. Tell God what you need, and thank him for all he has done.* (Philippians 4:6)

On the other hand, sometimes situations come into our lives that truly have the potential to shake us to our core. Uncertainty about our future, the death of a loved one, major problems with our spouse, an unexpected illness or trouble with our kids are just a few examples of the many things that can throw us off course. As long as you and I live on this earth, we will have to deal with difficulties, but:

*It is possible to survive the storms of life unscathed if you have the right foundation.*

When the storms of life hit, bringing fear, uncertainty and even desperation, the first and most important thing you can do is to make sure you are building your life on a solid foundation.

## PRINCIPLE I:
## SECURE A SOLID FOUNDATION

Whether you realize it or not, you are building your life on some sort of foundation—a foundation that reflects whatever it is you have faith in. And you do have faith in something. We all do; we all have a set of beliefs through which we filter the world. Over time, those beliefs, whether positive or negative, build our foundation.

Take a minute to seriously consider the question: *What do you have faith in?* Who do you have faith in? Yourself? Your spouse? Your business partners? A religious tradition? Karma? The universe? An ephemeral God? What kind of faith foundation are you building your life on? When the wind starts whipping outside your window, how do you stay grounded?

Jesus once told a story about two different types of people—one who is constantly blown around by the storms of life and another who is always able to stand, no matter what the circumstances:

> *Anyone who listens to my teaching and follows it is wise, like a person who builds a house on solid rock. Though the rain comes in torrents and the floodwaters rise and the winds beat against that house, it won't collapse because it is built on bedrock. But anyone who hears my teaching and doesn't obey it is foolish, like a person who builds a house on sand. When the rains and floods come and the winds beat against that house, it will collapse with a mighty crash.* (Matthew 7:24-27)

When your faith is built on the right foundation, you can face life's problems—from the smallest worries to the biggest tragedies—without being shaken. But if you put your faith in the wrong place, you will struggle when difficult circumstances come your way and, all too often, collapse completely when the strong storms of life start raging.

As I mentioned in the Introduction, Hurricane Bob was my first lesson in the fact that having the right foundation is essential to being able to ride out a storm unscathed. But at that point in my life, I didn't know what the right foundation was. It wasn't until several years later that I discovered the truth that so many before me have known: The only foundation worthy of building on, and the only one strong enough to weather life's storms, is the foundation of faith in God and his son, Jesus Christ. In the Gospels, Jesus himself says:

> *I am the way, the truth, and the life. No one can come to the Father except through me.* (John 14:6)

Later, he asks his own disciples—people who had walked with him for years, seen him perform miracles, and listened to his teaching and his claims—this:

> *Who do you say that I am?* (Mark 8:29)

Eventually, we all have to answer the same question. We all have to make a decision about who we believe Jesus is.

## Who Is This Jesus?

There are really only two possible answers. Either we fully embrace Jesus as who he says he is, or we reject his teachings totally and continue on our way. There is no middle ground. Take a look at how Cambridge University professor and former agnostic C.S. Lewis once positioned the options:

> *I am trying here to prevent anyone saying the really foolish thing that people often say about Him: 'I'm ready to accept Jesus as a great moral teacher, but I don't accept His claim to be God.' That is the one thing we must not say. A man who was merely a man and said the sort of things Jesus said would not be a great moral teacher. He would either be a lunatic—on a level with the man who says he is a poached egg—or else he would be the Devil of Hell. You must make your choice. Either this man was, and is, the Son of God: or else a madman or something worse. You can shut Him up for a fool, you can spit at Him and kill Him as a demon; or you can fall at His feet and call Him Lord and God. But let us not come with any patronizing nonsense about His being a great moral teacher. He has not left that open to us. He did not intend to.[1]*

1   Lewis, C. S. *Mere Christianity*. London: The MacMillan Company, 1952. p. 40-41

When you and I acknowledge Jesus as the son of God and accept the free gift of salvation that God has offered through him (John 3:16), we gain forgiveness for our sins, a relationship with the one who created us, and eternity in heaven. If you are ready to invite Jesus into your life, or if you'd like some more information for study, go to www.BeUnshakable.com. To read more about my personal story of faith, turn to the Epilogue.

With Jesus as your solid foundation, it is possible to remain unshakable no matter what kind of storms you face. Throughout the Scriptures, God has said he will give you unshakable faith, as you trust him with your life. In fact, he has committed to even more than that; he will give you peace, power, protection and a plan when things go wrong. Let's take a look at each of those four promises in detail.

## Peace: God will give you peace when you are anxious.

Remember the Scripture I mentioned earlier in this chapter that says not to be anxious about anything? Those words were written by the Apostle Paul, a man who faced intense persecution in his lifetime. He actually wrote the verses from a prison cell, in the form of a letter to the Christians in the city of Philippi. After instructing his readers not to worry, Paul goes on to say that when we focus our attention on God, God will give us his peace:

> *Don't worry about anything; instead, pray about everything. Tell God what you need, and thank him for all he has done. Then you will experience God's peace, which exceeds anything we can understand. His peace will guard your hearts and minds as you live in Christ Jesus.* (Philippians 4:6-7)

Paul is simply expounding on Jesus' earlier words to a group of scared disciples:

> *Peace be with you.* (John 20:19)

Those four words have the ability to wipe away your worries and anxieties and replace them with assurance, if you understand their power and lean into them as Paul describes.

The same God who created the galaxies, formed the heavens and the earth and knew you before you were born invites you to rest in his strength. His son, Jesus, who raised the dead, caused blind men to see and overcame the grave is the same one who says to you and me (and I paraphrase), "Hey, give your problems to me." In Matthew, he (actually) says:

> *Come to me, all of you who are weary and carry heavy burdens, and I will give you rest.* (Matthew 11:28)

Given his resumé, I believe he's capable of handling our burdens. But we have to take the intentional step of giving them to him. When we do, he promises to replace our anxiety with peace.

## Power: God will give you power when you are weak.

Have you ever met someone who has it all together? Let me confirm something you may have suspected: That togetherness is 90% façade. None of us has everything under control. The people who act like they don't have a worry in the world are usually just hiding the truth behind a carefully constructed exterior. They may impress us, but they don't impress God; he sees the reality. God is drawn instead to people who are willing to admit their weakness and rely on him. Why? Because those are the people he can give his power to. The Bible is filled with example after example of imperfect, ordinary, weak people who God uses to do extraordinary things.

> *The same God who created the galaxies, invites us to rest in his strength.*

When we try to match wits with life's storms in our own power, we get beaten down pretty quickly. We can call on all of our resources and strength but, in the end, what we have just isn't enough—something we can all attest to if we are honest with ourselves. Hiding our failure behind a forced smile doesn't make anything better. But when we are willing to admit our weakness and acknowledge God's strength, we start finding our footing on the solid foundation he provides. As Paul writes:

> *I can do everything through Christ who gives me strength.* (Philippians 4:13)

Why would we even want to operate in our own limited strength when we have access to God's unlimited power?

## Protection: God will give you protection when you are afraid.

Fear is the most common of all human emotions. Every single one of us is afraid of something—sometimes with good reason, sometimes without. What are you afraid of? Is it something you're facing tomorrow? Something next year? Is it a financial problem? A health crisis? The loss of a relationship? Whatever you are afraid of, God is willing and able to stand as your protector in the face of that fear.

Our culture perpetuates a misguided image of God. Too often, he is depicted as a feeble, white-haired old man who would seem to have little control over this spinning mass of earth. That image is completely wrong. Scripture paints the real picture:

> *The Lord is my rock, my fortress, and my savior; my God is my rock, in whom I find protection. He is my shield, the power that saves me, and my place of safety.* (Psalm 18:2)

A great warrior named David wrote these words. Every day, David faced the kind of fear and tragedy you and I can only imagine, or maybe get a glimpse of through Hollywood epics. Still, he understood that God was his protector. In the same way that God protected David, he stands ready to protect you, no matter what you are facing.

## Plan: God will give you a plan when you are uncertain.

Uncertainty is a telling state of being. When the storms of life create uncertainty, you and I have a choice: we can either become insecure or we can look to God for direction. What we choose is a good indicator of the strength of our foundation. When we are not standing on solid rock, our natural tendency is to face uncertainty with an arrogance that both stems from insecurity and breeds more insecurity. We pull inside ourselves and think, "I can handle this. I have the bank account/the education/the title/the intelligence (take your pick). I'll figure it out." The irony is that facing uncertainty with this kind of perspective only brings greater uncertainty, by piling more weight on a faulty foundation.

On the other hand, uncertainty can cause us to look to God. And since he is the one who knows our future and knows how our story plays out in the end, he's the best one to look to:

> *"For I know the plans I have for you," says the LORD. "They are plans for good and not for disaster, to give you a future and a hope."* (Jeremiah 29:11)

God has the master plan for your life and mine. All we have to do is ask him for it. Consider what the disciple James says about tapping into God's plan:

> **You can survive the storms of life if you have the right foundation.**

*If you need wisdom, ask our generous God, and he will give it to you. He will not rebuke you for asking.* (James 1:5)

No matter what is causing uncertainty in your life, God has a plan for your peace and well-being on the other side of it. You can find your confidence by looking to him.

## THE RIGHT FOUNDATION

When you put your faith in Jesus as the foundation for your life—rather than putting it in family, friends, yourself, your work or anything else—God will give you his peace, his power, his protection and his plan. Only then will you be unshakable no matter what comes your way. When things go wrong, you won't be anxious. You'll let yourself rely on God's strength. You'll have the confidence and poise to move forward knowing that he is protecting you, and you will trust his plan for your future. From such a foundation of faith, you'll be able to sleep soundly through every dark night no matter how fiercely the winds whip just outside your window.

# ACKNOWLEDGEMENTS

**Nelson Searcy:** I would first like to express my eternal thanks to Jesus Christ, God's Son, for the eternal breakthrough He worked in my life when He called me to Himself during my freshman year of college. Thank you, God!

For this book, I must express my appreciation to C.A. Meyer, a former member and group leader at The Journey Church. This is the second book we have co-authored together (*At the Cross: With the People Who Were There* was our first best-selling collaboration). While my gifts are more on the "logic side," her gifts are more on the "creative side," and this made for a great writing partnership.

Equally, I must thank my long-time collaborator and co-author Jennifer Dykes Henson for her immense contribution to this book. Jennifer too is a former member and group leader at The Journey Church, along with her husband, Brian, and their two girls. I've lost count of the dozen-plus books that we have worked on together, and yet I'm constantly amazed at how Jennifer continues to up her game. And while she worked mainly "behind the scenes" in this book, her input, advice and editing have made it much stronger and far more accessible.

And speaking of "behind the scenes," it takes a lot for a book to go from concept to completion. It's no understatement to say that this book would not exist beyond a file on my Macbook without the exceptional management and guidance of Sandra Olivieri, vice president at Church Leader Insights. Her gentle hand guided this project from start to finish. Using her management, creative, copywriting and journalism skills, she made the content of the book stronger and the physical/e-book a reality. Thank you, Sandra.

Many others contributed to this book as well. While the idea of "Breakthrough" was mine, it was originally the teaching team at The Journey Church who helped me bring the ideas alive, led by my long-time colleagues Pastor Kerrick Thomas and Pastor Jason Hatley—who both continually push themselves to deeper engagement with Scripture, inspirational communication and personal growth. Special thanks to Raelyn Garriga, my long-time executive assistant, for her sharp eye in proofreading and assistance with scriptural and general research.

A special thanks to all of those who read the manuscript and offered insights, too many to name, but I'm thankful for each of you. The book is stronger for their comments but any errors, theologically and grammatically, are mine alone.

Finally, my writing ministry—which now stretches to over 20 books—would not be possible without my family's commitment. I write during discretionary times, as my primary ministry is The Journey Church, so my wife, Kelley, and son, Alexander, have to deal with my early morning writing habits, odd hours locked away in my home office and occasional requests for just a few more minutes "while I wrap up this section." As soon as I sent this book off to print, my wife and I immediately left for a two-week celebration of our 30th wedding anniversary (yes, we married young—ha). Likewise, right as I was completing this book, my son had a trifecta of big events: graduating high school, turning 18 and securing his third-degree black belt in Kenpo Karate. Personally, I celebrated two health-related milestones as I wrapped up this book: five-plus years cancer-free and two years post-liver transplant. The Lord has provided my health breakthrough. My health is being fully restored and I'm grateful for this "bonus time" for as long as it lasts. I am blessed beyond measure.

**C.A. Meyer:** Thank you to the God who saves, redeems and restores. Jesus Christ is our breakthrough, and may He receive all the glory. Thank you to Nelson, Sandra and the Church Leader Insights team for inviting me to assist with this project, which I pray encourages all who read it to trust in God and His Word through every season.

**Jennifer Dykes Henson:** My partnership with Nelson Searcy over close to two decades has been nothing short of incredible. I am continually humbled and excited to be part of what God is doing through him. Thank you, Nelson, for inviting me into this magnificent endeavor.

Thanks to my husband, Brian, for being a constant well of love and encouragement, and for continually challenging me to live a life worthy of the work I've been called to. And to my two daughters, Isabelle and Ivey-Grace: My life's goal is to engage in the world in a way that will make you proud and that will model for you the fullness of life that Jesus offers us all. You are my inspiration.

Finally, I thank God for once again giving me the opportunity to engage in meaningful work that will, hopefully and prayerfully, impact the lives of those who find it in their hands.

# ABOUT NELSON SEARCY

Dr. Nelson Searcy is the Founding and Lead Pastor of The Journey Church, with locations across New York City and in Boca Raton, Florida, where he lives with his wife, Kelley, and son, Alexander. Nelson is a cancer survivor and the author of over 20 books, including the Revised and Updated edition of

*The Greatness Principle: Finding Significance and Joy by Serving Others, The New You,* and *The Generosity Ladder: Your Next Step to Financial Peace.* See **www.NelsonSearcyBooks.com** for more. After becoming a Christian in college, Nelson entered full-time ministry in 1990. He has served with Rick Warren at Saddleback Church in Southern California. Today Nelson and The Journey Church appear routinely on lists such as "The 50 Most Influential Churches" and "The 25 Most Innovative Leaders." As founder of ChurchLeaderInsights.com, he's trained more than 50,000 church leaders, with over 3,000 of them being church planters. Nelson holds a BA and BS from Gardner Webb University, MDiv from Duke University and DLitt from Louisiana Baptist University. His continued mission is to help church leaders and church members around the world cooperate with God to fulfill the Great Commission.

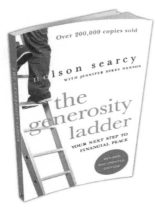
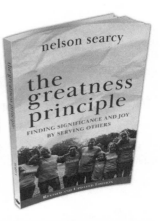

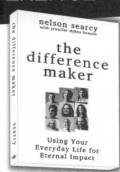

# BOOKS BY NELSON SEARCY

**Brand New!**

**The Greatness Principle:**
**Finding Significance**
**and Joy by Serving Others**
**(Revised & Updated)**
Topics: Ministry, Volunteers

**The Generosity Secret:**
**How to Get Out of Debt**
**and Find Financial Freedom**
Topic: Stewardship

**The New You**
Topics: Health,
Spiritual Growth

**Top seller!**

**At the Cross:**
**With the People**
**Who Were There**
Topics: Easter,
Spiritual Growth

**10th Anniversary!**

**Maximize:**
**How to Develop**
**Extravagant**
**Givers in Your Church**
Topic: Stewardship

**The Renegade Pastor's**
**Guide to Managing**
**the Stress of Ministry**
Topic: Leadership

**The Renegade Pastor's**
**Guide to Time**
**Management**
Topic: Leadership

**Best seller!**

**Fusion: Turning First-Time**
**Guests Into Fully-Engaged**
**Members of Your Church**
Topic: Assimilation

**10th Anniversary!**

**Activate: An Entirely**
**New Approach to**
**Small Groups**
Topic: Small Groups

**The Renegade Pastor:**
**Abandoning Average in**
**Your Life and Ministry**
Topic: Leadership

**The Generosity Ladder:**
**Your Next Step to**
**Financial Peace**
Topic: Stewardship

**Revolve: A New Way**
**to See Worship**
Topic: Worship
Planning

These books are available at Amazon.com and ChristianBook.com
For other resources, visit www.ChurchLeaderInsights.com

# A PERSONAL NOTE FROM THE AUTHOR

As a cancer survivor, transplant recipient and overachiever when it comes to having major surgeries, I invite you to consider these steps:

 **1) Regular blood donation.**
Visit this website: **RedCross.org/give-blood**

 **2) Organ donation.** You can potentially help up to seven people, and I know it's a prayerful decision. Learn more at **OrganDonor.gov**

 **3) Getting screened as early and as often as you can for all kinds of cancer.**
Develop a regular plan with your family doctor and dermatologist. Almost 40% of Americans will be diagnosed with cancer during their lifetimes.

Honor God with your body,

*Nelson*

*Don't you realize that your body is the temple of the Holy Spirit, who lives in you and was given to you by God? You do not belong to yourself, for God bought you with a high price. So you must honor God with your body.* (1 Corinthians 6:19-20 NLT)